Research Studies in Library Science, No. 10

RESEARCH STUDIES IN LIBRARY SCIENCE
Bohdan S. Wynar, Editor

No. 1.   *Middle Class Attitudes and Public Library Use.* By Charles Evans, with an Introduction by Lawrence Allen.

No. 2.   *Critical Guide to Catholic Reference Books.* By James Patrick McCabe, with an Introduction by Russell E. Bidlack.

No. 3.   *An Analysis of Vocabulary Control in Library of Congress Classification and Subject Headings.* By John Phillip Immroth, with an Introduction by Jay E. Daily.

No. 4.   *Research Methods in Library Science. A Bibliographic Guide.* By Bohdan S. Wynar.

No. 5.   *Library Management: Behavior-Based Personnel Systems. A Framework for Analysis.* By Robert E. Kemper.

No. 6.   *Computerizing the Card Catalog in the University Library: A Survey of User Requirements.* By Richard P. Palmer, with an Introduction by Kenneth R. Shaffer.

No. 7.   *Toward a Philosophy of Educational Librarianship.* By John M. Christ.

No. 8.   *Freedom versus Suppression and Censorship.* By Charles H. Busha, with an Introduction by Peter Hiatt, and a Preface by Allan Pratt.

No. 9.   *The Role of the State Library in Adult Education: A Critical Analysis of Nine Southeastern State Library Agencies.* By Donald D. Foos, with an Introduction by Harold Goldstein.

No. 10. *The Concept of Main Entry as Represented in the Anglo-American Cataloging Rules. A Critical Appraisal with Some Suggestions: Author Main Entry vs. Title Main Entry.* By M. Nabil Hamdy, with an Introduction by Jay E. Daily.

No. 11. *Publishing in Switzerland: The Press and the Book Trade.* By Linda S. Kropf.

The Concept of Main Entry
as Represented in the
Anglo-American Cataloging Rules

A Critical Appraisal with Some Suggestions:

Author Main Entry vs. Title Main Entry

M Nabil Hamdy

Introduction by
Jay E. Daily
Professor of Library and Information Science
University of Pittsburgh

1973

LIBRARIES UNLIMITED, INC., LITTLETON, COLO.

TABLE OF CONTENTS

CHAPTER V – LITERARY UNITS (cont'd.)

**CHAPTER VI – THE EFFECT OF THE MAIN ENTRY PRINCIPLE
ON THE RULES FOR THE CHOICE OF ENTRY**

CHAPTER VII – TITLE UNIT ENTRY

LIST OF ILLUSTRATIONS

LIST OF TABLES

ACKNOWLEDGMENTS

The author wishes to express his gratitude to his advisor and the chairman of the Dissertation Committee, Dr. Jay E. Daily, for his guidance and encouragement. Thanks are also due to the members of the Doctoral Committee: Professor Allen Kent, Drs. Frank Sessa, Harold Lancour, John Singleton and especially Dr. Phillip Immroth for his helpful suggestions.

A special word of thanks is due to Dr. Elaine Svenonius, who guided me through my writing period, has cheerfully and patiently edited the manuscript and made valuable suggestions. For editing the final version the author is indebted to Dr. Robert Stueart.

Finally, I wish to thank my wife Amira and our two sons, Khaled and Omar, whose patience, sacrifice and understanding during the research and writing provided me with a constant source of reassurance.

INTRODUCTION

In *Le Sang d'un Poete*, Jean Cocteau observes that he who destroys a statue runs the risk of becoming one himself. The author of this book is so endangered. Although chopping the first chapter of the *Anglo-American Cataloging Rules* of 1967 into fine pieces is praiseworthy, the author does not stop at that. He achieves even a far more important goal than substantiating title unit entry, or standard bibliographic description, as a method of processing. Leaving aside the fact that this dissertation will serve as a measure of excellence for the clarity of its prose and for the validity of its method, this book is a landmark in cataloging theory because it firmly establishes descriptive cataloging as part of the process of a library and not merely the fascinating sport of catalogers.

My own introduction to title unit entry came as a question posed by Ms. Helen Becker when she was a part-time cataloger and I was assistant director for technical services of the University of Pittsburgh libraries. Instructed in the "red rules," the 1949 portion of the Anglo-American Code, I was constantly searching for a method that would avoid the tortuous perplexities of establishing main entry. My contribution was "The Mandalay Rules," used with great success during the time I was in Burma. Ms. Becker asked, as nearly as I can remember the question, "Why not enter everything under title and make such other entries as will best serve the public?" At that time Mr. Hamdy was working as a searcher for the head of acquisitions, and he was also the first of my advisees in the doctoral program. He was unfortunately at the mercy of circumstances that determined a lengthy and frustrating timetable for his work, and he progressed from searcher to the head of the cataloging department as I undertook full-time teaching and the development of areas of research in the program of doctoral studies.

While many others became interested in and contributed to the sum of our knowledge, only the patient dissection of the rules for choice of entry could establish title unit entry as a method of processing both competent and efficient. The work published here is rather like those conclusive statements of renaissance science that located the soul not in the human frame but in the human spirit. The author of this work may face the wrath of the medievalists among our fellow professional catalogers. At the least, the publication of this book should encourage a complete reappraisal of our cataloging methods, because the difference between title unit entry and author-equivalent unit entry, a confabulation of main and unit entry arising from tradition rather than practicality, can be clearly seen not only in the job classifications and

11

job descriptions of cataloging departments, but also in our philosophy of librarianship.

The work of descriptive cataloging can be done by library technical assistants if a title unit entry method is employed, but only a professional who gains a mystical understanding of main entry as a system of preferences can hope to catalog as his fellows elsewhere do. Even at that, wherever a choice is possible—and no matter how slight the differences—even catalogers of unimpeachable precision will not think alike. In fact, one cataloger may have different ideas on different occasions. It is as if the number of angels dancing on the point of a needle were determined by strict rules capable of many varying interpretations. Yet the *Anglo-American Cataloging Rules* have been accepted as the measure of standardization and professionalism, somewhat like canon law. The choice of main entry has been offered as the scholarly part of descriptive cataloging to be attempted only by those who have been ordained by graduate education.

A true concern for the user, rather than for the pride of the cataloger, would lead to the obvious solution of making entries equivalent, of destroying the mystical distinction between main and added entries. With pieces of information as his guide, the user does not care how he finds the work he seeks so long as his search can be brief and effective. I have long contended that a rule requiring that main entry be established for the person or corporate body "responsible" for the work demands a metaphysical judgment on the part of the cataloger. While the result of the choice may gratify the cataloger, the delay and expense in coming to something that satisfies a nice sense of professionalism is wasteful. Meanwhile, other important work is not done for lack of time: subject analysis is scant and shallow, analytics are considered a luxury, and some material gets indefinitely postponed, whether or not this frustrates a user. In plain terms, the choice of main entry is a professionals' puzzle which has neither meaning nor importance in the overall scheme of the catalog.

An administrator cannot afford to care whether the cataloger's sense of scholarly achievement is coddled by the rules he uses. A cataloger must be judged by results—by shelved books available for use and accessible through the catalog in all the forms that the users can be expected to need. At a time when technology could make the process fast without sacrificing quality, there is no excuse for delays caused by esthetic quibbling over choice of entry—especially since only another cataloger can appreciate the exquisite results. Daniel Gore's vituperations about catalogers appear to be justified: like Canon Teep's wife in the story by Saki, presently they invite a certain amount of cruelty. Until someone was intelligent, persistent, and brave enough to undertake the fiercely difficult task of explaining the rules objectively, of tracing each detail until its lack of consistency and meaning was apparent, we had only a body of rules of venerable antecedents which served, even if they did not serve well. With this book, however, we can discover what cataloging is all about. It restores our sense of direction as catalogers and establishes a perspective that is worldwide and looks to the future. For that reason I am confident that the profession will agree that this doctoral dissertation is a landmark much needed in the wasteland of cataloging theory.

Of some dissertations it can be said that the chief value lay in the effort the candidate expended in completing his work; of others, that a small problem has been resolved or an interesting fact run to earth. A few have established a new field of investigation and a method of surveying it. This work is truly a dissertation accomplishing what all the others have aimed for and justifying the doctorate in library science. It is very gratifying to me, not because I had an easy job as advisor nor because the author is one of the best of good men, but because I could say that my student has surpassed me, my efforts have been a success, my work justified, and my beliefs and speculations given a firm reference point. I usually advise doctoral candidates that while a dissertation is expected to advance knowledge they must be content with a few millimeters. This dissertation reflects kilometers of progress. I am very grateful that I could be aboard when the goal was reached.

University of Pittsburgh   Jay F. Daily
September 17, 1972

CHAPTER I

ANGLO-AMERICAN CATALOGING RULES

... there is a factorial order which applies in every section of librarianship and in every operation, not least in the Cataloging Department. In order of importance, the factors are: 1, The user, the reader, the inquirer; 2, The document, the book, the record; 3, The economy, as represented by the least effort for the greatest benefit; 4, The system by which the user and the document are brought together with the least effort and the greatest benefit; 5, The staff, through whom the system operates.

We must analyze our own personal reactions quite honestly when faced with any proposal for the improvement of our work, and we should measure the results against such a philosophy as is prescribed here.

A. C. Downing

General Background

Libraries today find that for the vast and rapidly growing volume of recorded information under bibliographic control, the traditional card catalog has become an inadequate tool because methods of cataloging have not kept pace. The profession has been reevaluating its methods and exploring new techniques for self-improvement. Data processing equipment has been introduced and exploited in various library operations, and the present and future impact of this new technology on the process of cataloging is noticeable everywhere. The Library of Congress MARC Project is opening new avenues toward cooperative cataloging and exchange of bibliographic information both inside and outside the United States. MARC data bases are now used for the production of book catalogs, bibliographies, and catalog cards in various places in the United States. Networks such as the Ohio College Library Center (OCLC), the New England Library Network (NELINET) and MARC Oklahoma are examples of developments where MARC tapes are used. The files of OCLC presently can be searched and cards can be ordered through terminals placed in remote locations. The success of automated systems will have far-reaching implications on the future of catalogs and cataloging; certainly it will make the cataloging process more efficient and the catalog a more serviceable instrument for its users.

Cataloging rules, in their period of development, have gone through a period of investigation and inquiry on national and international levels. These efforts culminated in the publication of the *Anglo-American Cataloging Rules*, 1967, hereafter referred to as the *AACR*. Criticisms of these rules are based on their deviation from the *Paris Principles*,[1] on their length and complication,[2] and on their lack of regard for the new technology and its computer applications.[3] Some criticisms suggest the need for simplified or abridged editions of the rules,[4] while others ask for a complete revision.[5] As a matter of fact, the rules have been under continuous revision since their publication. Amendments to the rules were issued by the Library of Congress in its *Cataloging Information Bulletin* and by the Library Association in its *Catalogue & Index*. Still more changes to the rules have been proposed by the Library of Congress.

Like its predecessors, the *AACR* is based on the principle of main entry under author for the construction of multiple-entry catalogs. The functions of these catalogs are similar to the functions for which the earlier codes were designed. This principle seems to be the cause of the continuous criticisms and revisions of the cataloging rules. Developed during the nineteenth century to provide an economic means of constructing the book catalog, the rules seem to be ambiguous, inconsistent, and unnecessarily complicated. The replacement of the book catalog with the card catalog, and the replacement of the individually prepared entry with the unit card, have effectively destroyed the main entry's claim of economy.

Currently the validity of establishing the main entry under author is being questioned and challenged, and the title unit entry is being suggested as a substitute. The literature on this subject affirms that the latter approach will make the cataloging rules more consistent and less ambiguous. Where adopted, there would no longer be the question, "What is the main entry?"

Whether the title unit entry should be accepted is a still-unresolved question which requires intensive investigation and study. Jay E. Daily expresses this need in his following statement:

> . . . as a topic for research of the most practical kind, we are left wondering whether the unit card ought not to be a title entry. Much would be solved that is now problematic in automated methods of cataloging. This idea was advanced . . . to the author and so far he has found no way to disprove the hypothesis that title entry as unit entry is most readily adapted to all purposes in the library.[6]

It is generally agreed that the major functions of a library catalog are: 1) to enable a user to find a book of which the author or the title is known, and 2) to show what the library has by a given author and what editions the library has of a given work. It is desirable that the cataloging rules should result in entries that further these functions and make the catalog an efficient tool.

The present study has been designed to explore the theoretical and logical foundations of the principle of main entry and to establish whether or not this principle should be included in a cataloging code designed to fulfill the above-stated functions of a catalog. More specifically, the study examines the bases of those rules in the *AACR* that deal with the choice of entry, to determine if the substitution of title entry for main entry is possible and desirable from a sound theoretical principle. This study consists of, first, a descriptive investigation of the origins of both the main entry and the title entry, and second, a systematic analysis of the rules for the choice of entry in the first chapter of *AACR* in order to disclose any ambiguities, inconsistencies, or complexities. The third phase of the study provides a model cataloging code for the title unit entry, to which some examples are applied to show how the rules function.

Much of the discussion on the revision of the *AACR*, being largely opinion and debate, is not relevant to this examination of the principles on which the present rules stand. A demand for revision raises the question whether a new approach is not the easiest solution to the problems. If not, then perhaps the present study can clarify the issue of what sections are most in need of revision.

FOOTNOTES

[1] Andrew D. Osborn, "AA Cataloging Code," review of *Anglo-American Cataloging Rules*, North American text, in *Library Journal*, XCIII (October 1, 1968), 3523-25; James A. Tait, *Authors and Titles; an Analytical Study of the Author Concept in Codes of Cataloguing Rules in the English Language, from that of the British Museum in 1841, to the Anglo-American Cataloguing Rules, 1967* (Hamden, Conn.: Archon Books, 1969; London: Clive Bingley, Ltd., 1969), p. 139; Andre Nitecki, review of *Anglo-American Cataloging Rules*, in *American Documentation*, XVIII (October 1967), 255-57.

[2] "Revising the Rules," *Catalogue & Index*, No. 20 (October 1970), 3.

[3] Osborn, "AA Cataloging Code," p. 3525; Theodore C. Hines, review of *Anglo-American Cataloging Rules*, in *College & Research Libraries*, XXIX (January 1968), 63.

[4] "Revising the Rules," p. 3.

[5] Hines, review of *Anglo-American Cataloging Rules*, p. 63.

[6] Jay E. Daily, "Binder's Title," *Encyclopedia of Library and Information Science* (New York: Marcel Dekker, 1969), II, 485.

CHAPTER II

CHOICE OF ENTRY:
THEORIES AND PHILOSOPHY

Introduction

In reviewing the literature relating to the choice of entry, the cataloging student is faced with two different schools of thought—the so-called Oriental and Western schools. The first school subscribes to the concept of "title unit entry." According to this concept, entries begin with titles and no choice of entry is required; thus, rules for choice of entry are not required. Countries adopting this concept usually do not possess a set of cataloging rules, and, in particular, there are no rules for the selection of entries. Because the literature and documentation on the origins and theory of the Oriental school are meagre, little is known about it. The precepts of the school are followed by a few countries in Asia and the Middle East.

In contrast to the Oriental school, the Western school is based on the determination of authorship responsibility for the selection of a main entry. This school has a far larger representation with regard to the number of countries that accept its precepts. It is followed by the United States, the United Kingdom, many European, African, Asian, and Eurasian countries, and probably all the rest of the Americas. Two features characterize this school: first, it is divided in opinion as to what an author is. The Anglo-American school and its followers regard as authors corporate bodies as well as personal authors. On the other hand, the German school differs by preferring entry under title instead of corporate entry.[1]

The second feature characterizing the Western school is a well-developed body of cataloging rules to govern the process of selection and determination of entries. The function of these rules is to bring consistency and uniformity to catalog entries. This function has been recognized by the designers of cataloging codes since as early as 1852. Charles C. Jewett stated, "It should be remembered that the principle object of the rules is to secure uniformity; . . ."[2] Now, after more than 100 years, this function is still primary. Lubetzky writes:

> These rules are necessary and important for three reasons: 1) to expedite the work of cataloging—by providing for the cataloger ready directions to follow; 2) to insure uniformity and consis-

tency in the treatment of library materials—without which the catalog would tend to become increasingly chaotic and confusing; and 3) to facilitate bibliographic cooperation among libraries— and thus serve the cause of bibliographic and cataloging economy.[3]

The history of the Western school records many cataloging codes, the latest of which is the *Anglo-American Cataloging Rules* published in 1967. In 1939, J.C.M. Hanson published a comparative study of cataloging rules in various countries.[4] The study included nineteen codes for fourteen different countries, and this was merely a selection of codes regarded as most important at the time. The proliferation in the publishing of cataloging rules led Valter Ahlstedt to remark in 1950:

> In this age of rationalization it seems to be an enormous waste of time and labour for a great number of libraries to use different rules to catalogue a material of mostly the same kind.[5]

This proliferation, however, has not ceased. In a recent study, Eugene Hanson and Jay E. Daily cited forty-eight different codes for only twelve countries. But again this study was selective and did not cite all the cataloging codes in use in all countries of the world; all Asian codes were omitted. It is difficult to state even approximately the number of cataloging codes used in the various countries.[6] This is due to the fact that, in some cases, the rules do not even exist in published form. They survive only as informal written tradition.[7]

Despite the overwhelming acceptance of the main entry in the West, there have been several occasions in which the title unit entry, favored by the Oriental school, has been advanced in Western thinking for the purposes of achieving both international cooperation and uniformity in cataloging rules. In recent years, the title unit entry has been growing in favor in the Western world; many Western scholars advocate it as an alternative to the main entry. The remainder of this chapter will be devoted to exploring the history, theories, and merits of the Oriental and Western schools of thought. As was mentioned, there is a scarcity of literature on the title unit entry in the countries of its origin and predominate use. Consequently, the present discussion will be limited to those countries in the Middle East where a literature exists (particularly Egypt and other Arab countries). With regard to the Western school, the history of the main author entry will be discussed only briefly, since it already has been well covered in several studies.[8]

The Title Unit Entry

Definition

The title unit entry can be defined as a unit entry, without a main entry heading. It begins with the title and incorporates the complete bibliographic description of an item (e.g., monograph, serial, motion picture, filmstrip, phonorecord, picture, etc.). An author statement is always included in the bibliographic description. In addition to the bibliographic description subject headings and/or added entries are made for the author or authors of the published item. (See examples in Chapter VI.) The author is defined here as the person or corporate body responsible *fully* or *partially* for the creation of the intellectual or artistic content of a work—e.g., the writer of a book, the compiler of a bibliography, the composer of a musical work, the artist who paints a picture, or the photographer who takes a photograph.

When title unit entries are used, works are entered alphabetically by title under each of the headings in the catalog. For example, in the subject catalog works are listed alphabetically by title under each subject heading and not by author. In the author catalog, works are listed alphabetically by title under each author added entry. Also, depending on the library's policy regarding title entries, a title added entry may or may not be made for a given publication.

It should be noted that the title unit entry, like the main entry (to be defined later), is a complete record of an item. It differs from the main entry in only two ways:

1. It does not specify or prescribe one heading as the "main" entry. Rather, *all* the authors (personal or corporate) on the title page of an item are given added entries as required.
2. The authorship statement is always incorporated in the body of the description.

The term "title unit entry" is a recent one. It was coined by Jay E. Daily in the 1960s to describe a concept of long standing.[9] Over the years this concept has been given different names by different writers. Both Valter Ahlstedt and Muhammed el-Mahdi, for example, referred to it as the "basic card."[10] A. E. Jeffreys called it an "alternative entry."[11] And more recently Warren B. Hicks and Alma M. Tillin referred to it as the "title main entry."[12] Regardless of the discrepancy in terminology, there seems to be agreement on what is meant by this concept.

According to el-Mahdi, the title unit entry is a "card without heading."[13] It includes only the description of books or other materials beginning with the title, not as a main entry but as an item of the description which is written in the second indention and is always followed by the author statement. Subject entries and/or added entries are then made for the author, authors or other contributors according to whatever rules are used for the choice of the form of heading.[14]

The title unit entry is similarly described by Jeffreys, who states, ". . . the unit card contains no heading, and all the headings are typed above the body of the entry as required."[15] Wilma Radford characterizes title unit entry cataloging as "preparing entries without headings."[16] She later observes that in these entries, "the tracing note would be a record of all entries made for a book, instead of for all but one, as at present."[17]

Historical Background

Historically, the title unit entry is attributed to the Orient or the East. For many years and "even today in the Orient the traditional entry for a book is its title."[18] China, Japan until recently, and some of the Arab countries, especially Egypt, are examples of the nations adopting this concept. Japan, it might be noted, changed from the title unit entry concept to the main entry concept when its rules were revised in 1953.[19]

In the Arab world it is suggested that the lack of family names in modern Arabic or Islamic names is a reason for the use of a title unit entry rather than a main author entry.[20] While this might be true, it is apparent from the literature that titles of books have always been favored over the names of their authors, even when there existed names similar to family names. Moreover, from early days, the titles of Arabic books have been structured in such a way as to make them distinctive and easy to remember.

Mahmoud el-Sheniti points out that:

> The general practice (initially set by the Egyptian National Library) has been to enter Arabic books under the title. The works of Arabic writers of the medieval period seem to have been known by their distinctive titles. The title overshadowed the name of the author, sometimes to the extent that in nineteenth century Iraq the families of Kashf al Gita' and al Gwahiri at Nejef took their names after titles of books written by their founders, on Shiite theology and on the Koran.[21]

el-Mahdi also remarks on the distinctiveness of Arab titles:

> The early [Arab writers] have always tried to make the title distinctive by adding to it a special element. In many cases, this element was a statement which was unrelated to the subject of the book, or the distinction was through rhyme.[22]

el-Mahdi goes on to point out that for modern titles of Arabic books the rhyme element has virtually disappeared—except in rare instances such as religious books, which sometimes appear with titles constructed according to the old tradition. The method of distinguishing through rhyme eventually was replaced by the addition of an element of peculiarity or curiosity. That is, authors began adopting titles which would attract readers. They were influenced in this respect by the headlines used in journalistic articles as well as by titles of motion pictures. Another influence was that publishers became artistic in the production of book jackets.[23]

The adoption of the title unit entry in the Arab countries has been given as the reason for the lack of modern cataloging rules similar to those used in the West.[24] Egypt, for example, does not have cataloging rules for the choice of main entry, since this need does not exist. It is as simple as that. As for descriptive cataloging, here the Anglo-American rules are usually followed. With regard to the form of heading, an authority list of medieval names is under development. The first draft of this list was published by el-Sheniti in 1961.[25] el-Mahdi recommends that modern names (after 1800) be entered under forenames. He believes that this will insure consistency and uniformity of practice. He also recommends that family names should be made obligatory in the names of every Arab.[26]

20

It has been advanced in the literature that the use of the title entry rather than the author entry in the East can be attributed in some way to the East's lack of emphasis on the importance of the individual.[27] This assumption lacks evidence and it is questionable whether it can really explain a cataloging tradition.

The Main Entry

Background

In the Western world the tradition favored by members of the library profession is to regard the choice of main entry as a problem of determination of authorship responsibility. In the West the main entry principle seems almost synonymous with author entry. The concept of author entry characterizes all the codes cited by Hanson and Daily. Although the concept was not formalized until the middle of the nineteenth century, when Anthony Panizzi defended his famous ninety-one rules, its roots extend back to 1595 and Andrew Maunsell's work, which represents the first formulation of a code of cataloging rules for authors. He insisted that one should be able to find books in the catalog under the surname of authors, translators, and subjects.[28] Since 1595 the author entry has steadily gained in prominence until now, in the twentieth century, it has become the basis for all cataloging rules in the West. Beginning in the Anglo-American cataloging rules of 1908 and in all subsequent codes to the present *AACR* 1967, the first basic rule, with minor variations in wording, has been "Enter a work under the name of its author,"[29] indicating that the main entry should be under the author of the work.

Definition

In defining the main entry, the codes are fairly similar. Charles A. Cutter was the first to introduce the term "main entry"; "The main entry, the full or principle entry."[30] Regarding the main entry, the 1908 Code was less flexible than Cutter. Here the main entry is defined as "The full or principle entry, as a rule the author entry."[31] Definitions given by later codes are more flexible than the 1908 definition. In this respect they are closer to Cutter's definition, but they are more elaborate. The 1949 rules define the main entry as:

> 1. The basic catalog card, usually the author entry, giving all the information necessary to the complete identification of a work. This entry bears also the tracings of all the other headings under which the work in question is entered in the catalog. It may bear in addition the tracing of related references and a record of other pertinent official data concerning the work.
> 2. The entry chosen for this main card, whether it be a personal or corporate name, the title of an anonymous work, a collection, composite work, periodical or serial, or a uniform title.[32]

21

As can be seen, this definition includes two meanings for main entry: 1) the "basic catalog card" and 2) the "heading" chosen for this card. The *AACR* 1967 definition similarly states:

> 1. The complete catalog record of a bibliographical entity, presented in the form by which the entity is to be uniformly identified and cited. The main entry normally includes the tracing of all other headings under which the record is to be presented in the catalog. 2. The heading under which such a record is presented in the catalog or, if there is no heading, the title.[33]

This definition is more flexible than any of its predecessors. In its first meaning it dispenses with the phrase "usually the author entry." Instead it uses the phrase "presented in the form by which the entity is to be uniformly identified and cited." By this modification, it recognizes the fact that the main entry is not usually the author entry. However, in its second meaning the definition still preserves the concept of the main heading. Since the underlying principle of the Code is that a work should be specified by its author and title (and by its title alone only in the case where it lacks an author). The implication is that a main entry under author is preferred to anything else.

Definitions of the main entry given by individual writers on the subject have not differed from those stated by the rules. It would seem that these writers have accepted unquestioningly the definitions provided by the rules. Margaret Mann, for example, defines the main entry as "the principle entry, usually the author entry: in a card catalog it is the entry from which all other entries are traced."[34] Similarly, Maurice F. Tauber states "the main entry is made under author or the person chiefly responsible when known, otherwise under title."[35] A more recent definition is that of Bohdan S. Wynar. According to him "the main entry is the basic catalog card; it is usually the author entry, giving all the information that identifies the work."[36]

From the definitions, it becomes obvious that the term "main entry" has been used, over the years, to refer to two different elements. The first element is the *record*, which contains the complete bibliographical description of an item. And the second element is the *main heading*, usually the author.

Obviously the main entry can be under something other than the author; for instance, it can be under the title. If this is the case, why then the insistence on the main entry under the author? In fact why should there be a main entry? In other words, what is the function of the main entry?

Function of the Main Entry

Much research and many studies have been devoted to the main entry. However, reasons for its existence are obscure and often confused. A. J. Wells points out that the notion of the main entry heading "has occupied more of our time to little purpose than anything else in librarianship. . . ."[37] Tait, in his *Authors and Titles*, studied historically the concept of author entry in the major cataloging codes in the English language. He found no progress towards

22

a better understanding or solution of the problems involved in this concept. He indicates that "in many respects, the earliest code, the British Museum code, is as modern as any of its successors."[38] Similarly, Daily and Myers state:

> Main entry turns out, in fact to be pretty much a will o' the wisp. It is a concept deeply imbedded in our practice, but when we come to inquire into the rationale behind it, it is difficult to discover any.[39]

In the literature several reasons have been suggested as being primarily responsible for the importance attached to the main entry and its reliance on the attribution of authorship responsibility. These reasons, however, seem to be largely based on unsubstantiated assumptions and emotional reactions. The *first* reason is that the author's name is the most important identification for a book. Henry A. Sharp states that the main author entry "is the most important entry we can make for a book. . . ."[40] However, Mr. Sharp gives no reason for this importance except tradition. Although he confesses that the author entry is not the only approach to a book, he states, "Nevertheless, most of us still stick to the established view that first and foremost comes the author entry."[41]

Similarly Julia Pettee points out:

> Books, in the Western world, are primarily associated with the man responsible for their creation. This is sound psychology from which there has been no important deviation. Where the author is an individual and the authorship is known, the personal entry under author, from the very beginning of European cataloging practice, has taken precedence over title or any other entry form. The form of entry for works without personal authors in evidence is still a matter upon which there is no general agreement in practice.[42]

The assumption that attribution of the authorship is of primary concern in determining the main entry is questionable. It is a fact that many books do not have authors, such as anonymous works, and many other books have more than one author responsible for their existence. Morever, many books now owe their existence to corporate bodies rather than to individual authors. It is also a fact that books are not always entered under their author; they are, for instance, entered under titles, form headings, uniform titles, corporate bodies, etc. Considerations such as these led Paul S. Dunkin to state that the main author entry is a convention which

> worked surely and smoothly only for a book with a single responsible author. For most books we find that the entry is often an arbitrary entry. For many books main entry is not 'usually the author entry'. . . . It is not impossible that to the user main entry means nothing so long as there is *some* entry under which he finds the book he wants. This is an age of increasing

23

multiple authorship and corporate authorship. Citation by author begins to lose favor in some areas.[43]

It is obvious, then, that the authorship responsibility is inadequate as the only criterion of determining the main entry of a book. It is impossible to rely upon it along in selecting entries or in constructing cataloging rules.

Books differ from one another, and no one set of rules can deal with all the possible variations. Often there is more than just one answer to a cataloging problem. However, the cataloger must choose only one: "If one were to catalog today the same group of books he cataloged a month ago, he would do no more than two-thirds of them in the same way he did them last month."[44] It is generally agreed that in many cases the same book is cataloged under different entries by different libraries and by different catalogers within the same library. An example is the following: The publication *Le Droit d'être un Homme: Recueil de textes préparés sous la direction de Jeanne Hersch* was published by UNESCO in 1968. It was entered by the Library of Congress (LC) under the compiler, Jeanne Hersch. In 1969 this publication was issued in English by the same organization, under the title *Birthright of Man*; it was entered by the same library under the entry "United Nations Educational, Scientific and Cultural Organization." Other examples of similar inconsistencies in cataloging are shown in Figures 1-6 below. Figures 1-2 are for publications entered by the same library (i.e., LC) under different entries. Figures 3-6 show different entries made by various libraries for identical publications.

FIGURE 1

a. LC Main Entry Under the Author
b. LC Main Entry Under the Title

—a.

```
Lewis, Sir William Arthur, 1915-
    Tropical development, 1880-1913: studies in economic
progress, edited by W. Arthur Lewis.  London, Allen &
Unwin, 1970.

    3-346 p.   23cm.  index.  £3.25          B 71-02799
```

```
Tropical development, 1880-1913. Edited by W. Arthur Lewis.
Evanston, Northwestern University Press, 1970.
    346 p.   23 cm.
```

b.—

FIGURE 2

FIGURE 2

a. LC Main Entry Under Author
b. LC Main Entry Under Compilor

—a.

Watt, James, 1736–1819.
    Partners in science: letters of James Watt & Joseph Black; edited with introductions and notes by Eric Robinson and Douglas McKie. London, Constable. 1970.
        xvi, 502 p. plates. facsims. 23 cm. index. 84/-   B 70–02857

b.—

Robinson, Eric, 1924–   comp.
    Partners in science; letters of James Watt and Joseph Black. Edited with introductions and notes by Eric Robinson and Douglas McKie. London, Constable 1970₎
        xvi, 502 p. facsims. 23 cm.   B***
        Includes James Watt's notebook of his experiments with heat: p. 431–479.

FIGURE 3

a. LC Main Entry Under Title
b. University of Pittsburgh Main Entry Under Editor

—a.

Survey of English dialects ₍edited₎ by Harold Orton and Eugen Dieth. ₍Leeds, Published for the University of Leeds by E. J. Arnold 1962–
        v. maps. 24 cm.

b.—

PE1705   Orton, Harold, 1898–   ed.
O 78   Survey of English dialects. Edited by Harold Orton and Eugen Dieth ₍and others₎ Leeds, Published for the University of Leeds by E.J. Arnold, 1962–
                    v. in maps, tables.

FIGURE 4

a. LC Main Entry Under Title
b. Main Entry Under Corporate Body
   NUC Entry Contributed by Yale University Law Library

—a.

The **Treatment** of offenders ₍by Robert Bessell and others₎.
London, Conservative Political Centre for the Bow Group,
1968.

40 p.   22 cm.   (A Bow Group pamphlet)   4/–   B 68–08111

b.—

Bow Group.
   The treatment of offenders ₍by Robert Bessell
and others.   London₎ Conservative Political
Centre for the Bow Group ₍1968₎
   1 v.   (CPC no. 388)

FIGURE 5

a. LC Main Entry Under Corporate Body
b. University of Pittsburgh Main Entry Under Title
c. NST Main Entry Under Title

—a.

Harvard University. *Graduate School of Business Admin-
istration.*
   Operating results of food chains.   1st–
1955–
Boston, Harvard University, Graduate School of Business
Administration, Division of Research.

   v.   illus.   28 cm.   annual.   (Harvard University.   Graduate
School of Business Administration.   Bureau of Business Research.
Bulletin)

b.—

qHD9321.2   Operating results of food chains.   1st-
O 61   1955–   Boston, Harvard University,
             Graduate School of Business Administra-
             tion, Division of Research ₍ etc.₎
                v.   illus.   annual.   (Harvard Univer-
             sity.   Graduate School of Business Admin-
             istration.   Bureau of Business Research.
             Bulletin, 148, 151, 154, 156, 162, 164,

FIGURE 5 (cont'd.)

```
         OPERATING RESULTS OF FOOD CHAINS.
         (CORNELL UNIVERSITY.  NEW YORK STATE
         COLLEGE OF AGRICULTURE) ITHACA. 1955-
            1955-  PUBLISHED AS HARVARD UNIVER-
            SITY.  GRADUATE SCHOOL OF BUSINESS
            ADMINISTRATION.  BUREAU OF BUSINESS
            ADMINISTRATION.  BULLETIN.
c.—
```

FIGURE 6

a. LC Main Entry Under Name of Symposium
b. British National Bibliography Main Entry
   Under Corporate Body

—a.

Symposium on Disorders of Language, *London, 1963.*
   Ciba Foundation Symposium: Disorders of Language;
   ₍proceedings₎ Edited by A. V. S. de Reuck and Maeve
   O'Connor. Boston, Little, Brown, 1964.

   xii, 356 p. illus. 21 cm.

```
         CIBA Foundation
              Symposium on disorders of language; edited
         by A.V.S. de Reuck and Maeve O'Connor.
         London, Churchill, 50/-.  Jan 1964. xii,356p.
         illus., tables, diagrs., bibliog.  21 cm.
         (Symposia)
                                          (B64-2613)
b.—
```

Looking in the *National Union Catalog* for works such as Festschriften, and works of multiple entry or shared authorship, one would be amazed by the variety of entries used by different libraries. To this effect Osborn writes:

> Anyone who analyses the entries contributed to a major union catalogue cannot but be impressed by the way in which competent cataloguers, with all the evidence before them, will interpret the evidence differently in selecting the main entry . . .[45]

This fact was also expressed quantitatively by other librarians who analyzed entries reported to a union catalog in Great Britain. Their analysis shows that forty libraries reported 224 different entries for thirteen books.[46]

This diversity of ways in which the main entry is selected for the same book, if it shows anything, expresses a lack of uniformity and standardization which supposedly is a prime objective of the main entry and the rules governing its choice. It also shows that the main entry is questionable as a standard for identifying bibliographic entries in single entry catalogs, as claimed by *AACR*.[47]

Inconsistency in choosing the main entry is the outcome of two factors: 1) the nature of the book and its title page and 2) the cataloging rules governing the choice of entry.

As to the first factor, books differ from one another in nature and complexity. Each book usually has its own unique title page describing its contents, and expressing the author's as well as the publisher's taste in the matter. Since the title page of a book is the major source of information about it, the variations between title pages of different books seriously affect the cataloging process and contribute to the diversity in description. M. Taube writes:

> Although it may seem at first glance that descriptive cataloging . . . is or should be a relatively simple and straight-forward affair, there are certain problems not always apparent to those who lack first hand experience with the difficulty of devising uniform entries from the haphazard information which appears on the title-pages of the various publications and reports requiring organization.[48]

A more eloquent comment, as well as an appeal for the standardization of title pages, is given by two British librarians:

> Efficient and consistent cataloging is largely dependent on the quality of the data supplied by the publication being cataloged. In this respect, the practice of many commercial publishers leaves much to be desired. We are all familiar with the problems raised by confusing and inconsistent edition statements; by variation in the names of authors and in titles between title pages, covers, dust jackets and half-title; by misprints and errors on the title page; and even by the occasional publication which is attributed to one author on the title page and to another on the cover. Such

defects are widespread throughout the whole range of trade and non-trade publications. No one wants to limit freedom of individual expression of publishers and typographers but a measure of standardization in publications would be of great advantage; and, since it is doubtful whether publishers themselves will generate their own standards, we should naturally look to the British Standards Institution—itself a publisher of long standing— to help in this matter. This help can come in two ways: first, by the establishment of an agreed set of recommendations, and second, by its setting an example of clarity and consistency in its own publications.[49]

In 1969 the International Organization for Standardization (ISO) approved its recommendation R1086-1969, Title-Leaves of Books, which was based on both the Indian Standard 790-793 and the draft British Standard Specification for the title leaves of a book, circulated in 1969.[50]

In the United States, the *American Standard for Title Leaves of a Book*, based on the above recommendation, was approved on March 31, 1971 and published by the American National Standards Institute, Inc., during the same year. The American Standard lists the essential information the leaf should contain, such as the title of the book; the title in the original language; the alternative or earlier title; the name of the author, compiler, and/or editor, personal or corporate; the name of the publisher; place of publication; the year of publication; etc. In addition, it provides amplified notes relating to the presentation of information for the publishers.[51] While it puts these notes in numerical order and distinguishes between the various kinds of information which should be placed either on the recto or verso of the title page, it does not indicate whether or not this numerical order must be followed consistently. For example, the author is listed as the first element of the note for the publisher. It is not evident from the Standard that the author's name must always be the first element on the title page. Whether or not such a standard or similar ones will be implemented and adopted will depend upon publishers; only time can tell.

Standardization of the title pages is important not only for efficient manual cataloging operations but also for eventual computer applications. It has been suggested that in the foreseeable future mechanized descriptive cataloging will be feasible. When effective direct optical character recognition techniques (OCR) become available the mechanical transcription of title pages will become a reality.[52]

The problems presented by OCR at this time are, however, complex. Present equipment cannot read "(1) proportional spacing, (2) non-standard fonts, or (3) special characters including diacritics."[53] What is required is improvement in the capabilities of the present equipment, improvements which are expected to come about in the 1970s; also required is standardization in the production of title pages with regard to format, fonts, etc. The latter requirement is a matter which even the recently approved American Standard has failed to take into consideration. Although such standardization is desirable, it is also impractical, because it would mean that all title pages of all books would have the same type faces and same format, a situation which would surely be unacceptable to both publishers and authors. The making of books is an art, and each publisher is concerned about the quality and esthetics of his books. The artistic quality of books is also of importance to book collectors and to persons in the book industry in general. Rather than requiring the standardization of title pages, a more practical as well as a more appropriate solution might be for each publisher to insert in each book an additional title page especially designed for OCR techniques. The information on the inserted page would be organized in a standardized format and the type face would be of a standard kind developed for OCR.

Variations in books and their title pages have a direct effect on cataloging rules in general. In constructing a cataloging code, special rules have to be designed to govern special cases. The more special cases there are, the larger is the number of rules and the larger is the chance for inconsistencies between rules. The ALA 1949 rules were criticized by Lubetzky for their large number.[54] The *AACR* 1967 rules tried to avoid this problem.

The second factor affecting inconsistency in choosing main entries are the rules themselves. It appears that there is no way to construct a set of simple, objective, and unbiased rules to handle all the diverse types of publications and their unique title pages. Throughout the history of cataloging rules, with the exception of the rules for simple publications of single authorship, choosing the main entry has been a rather complex process, one which in many cases has been subjected to value judgments based on arbitrary as well as sometimes biased decisions. Quite often the determination of main entry is a "guessing game."[55] While this problem will be discussed in more detail in Chapter VI, an example can be given now. In several rules in *AACR* 1967 the choice of entry is circumscribed by phrases such as "if there is doubt" or "in case of doubt." Phrases of this type are, of course, wide open to different interpretations. Thus, any cataloger can enter a publication under the entry he prefers and justify his decision by the fact that he is in doubt. Is the choice of main entry in this case a logical one?

Bias in selecting main author entries is apparent in our cataloging practice. For instance, in the case of works of shared authorship, the main entry usually favored is the first-named author, when the principal author is not indicated and there are no more than three authors named on the title page. This practice is considered by Lubetzky "both illogical and impractical."[56] He favors entry under title in this case and explains why.

> ... Logically, there is no apparent reason why this exception should be made for works of two or three authors, other than the weight of tradition. Practically, this exception entails problems when the order of the names differs on the title pages of the different editions, or when the authors are not named on the title page. To deal with these problems, special rules had to be provided.[57]

In addition to the problems Lubetzky points out, this case exemplifies a bias which librarians should not have to accept. In many cases the relation of each author to a multiple-authored book is the same. It can be that each of the authors has an equal share of intellectual responsibility, but the cataloger must select only one author and make the main entry. The other authors thus are relegated to a secondary level as added entries. Is this practice fair? Are we really providing main entries on the basis of fair intellectual responsibility?

Apart from its validity or invalidity, the main entry principle causes many practical problems in its everyday applications. To determine a main entry based on authorship responsibility is a complicated and time-consuming process. As Lubetzky indicates "to do so in such cases" as those shown above, one "would be flying in the face of overwhelming reality."[58] It requires much effort on the part of the cataloger, especially if the determination of entry requires extra bibliographical information not evident from the title page. Quite often the cataloger must search reference sources or look in other editions of a given publication to determine the main entry. The time and effort required to meet the specifications of the cataloging rules make them conflict with the first reason for their existence—that is, to expedite the work of cataloging. Margaret Mann considers "authorship determination" one of two major problems associated with the concept of author entry. She elaborates as follows:

> The author may be one or more persons; or authorship may be ascribed to a society or an institution. The identity of the author is usually revealed on the title page, but if it is not the cataloger must make a careful study of the preface and introduction in an attempt to discover the author. If no clue to the author is found, the title must be sought in other catalogs and in various reference works to see whether they record the same name of the person or body responsible for the work. Book reviews may help in this matter, but usually such information is not revealed if the author wishes to remain unknown.
>
> Frequently the determination of the author entry involves technicalities little realized by the uninitiated. It requires a knowledge of the various types of authorship based upon a definite code or rules. The student will find the selection of the correct entry is often difficult until he has mastered such a code with its suggestions for the possibilities of authorship.[59]

Surprisingly, given all the inconsistencies and complexities involved in determining main entries, there is a complete lack of studies showing how much time, effort, and money are involved in this determination. This is particularly unfortunate when we realize that these questionable main entries do not serve the needs of the users, either library patrons or staff. On the contrary, it can be said that they hinder the retrieval of the bibliographic information from our catalogs (a problem discussed later in this chapter).

The *second* reason for the importance attached to the main entry, which in the West is understood as the author entry, relates back to the practice of economics in the construction of book catalogs during the nineteenth century. Jay E. Daily and Mildred Myers tell us:

> Main entry is a concept which has come down to us directly from the book catalogs of the nineteenth century where it existed for purely economic reasons. All the information concerning a work was printed in one entry, which thus became the main entry, with the added or secondary entries containing only brief information under them. This was a sensible procedure to reduce the size of catalogs and therefore reduce production costs. The idea was carried over into the card catalog, and it is still the practice in some libraries where every card is typed for full information to be given in one entry, the main entry, and brief information only to be given in the added entries.[60]

Similarly, Dunkin writes:

> The printed catalog continues to influence our thinking even when we work with card catalogs. For instance, we talk of the "main entry: for a book even though (if we use printed cards or perhaps if we use typed cards) every card for that book is exactly alike. Apparently the notion that there is a "main entry" comes from definitions such as that by Cutter in which the "main entry" in a printed catalog is said to be "the full or principle entry" because this entry supplied contents and notes which may be omitted in other entries of the book under such things as subject or title.[61]

Also economics were observed in the early years of card catalogs when cards were produced manually in manuscript form. The cataloger had to make all the cards for a book, including main, added and subject entries. To save time and labor, the different cards varied in fullness. The main entry generally contained the fullest information, while on other cards some details were omitted to make them shorter. Thus, only one card for a book contained all the information necessary for complete bibliographical identification, while the other shorter cards served mostly the practical purpose of providing for additional access points.[62]

Now, with the prevalence of printed card catalogs using the unit card, and in the age of automation, the necessity for these time-saving practices no longer exists. As regards economic advantage, then, the principle of the main entry is unrealistic.

The unit card concept, introduced by the Library of Congress in 1901,[63] utilizes a basic card, complete with descriptive and bibliographical information, that is duplicated as required to provide added entries. Thus, each added entry card contains the information given on the main entry. For the users, the unit card concept puts before them a catalog, each entry of which is complete.[64] Eva Verona points out that in catalogs constructed according to the unit card concept, "the relation between the main entries and added entries is reduced to a more or less theoretical problem and will be less noticeable to the user."[65] The following is a similar view presented by a group of cataloging teachers.

> In most catalogs—dictionary, divided or classed—the main entry heading is only *one of several* approaches to a book. Patrons do not care what type of heading leads them to the book they want. They just want to find it quickly. To serve them it is as important to select correct *added* entry headings as it is to select the proper *main* entry heading.[66]

Another indication of the diminishing importance of the main entry in multiple entry catalogs using unit cards is the fact that many libraries disregard the main entry in filing their added entry cards. They interfile all main and added entries under the same author heading in one file, sub-arranged alphabetically by the title of the book. In fact, Rule 26B2 of the *ALA Filing Rules*, second edition, recommends this practice, stating:

> Interfile all main and added entries under the same author heading in one file. Subarrange alphabetically by the titles of books. On added entries, disregard an author main entry, but alphabet by the title main entry; also, disregard a uniform title when there is one and alphabet by the title page title.[67]

The advantages of this practice are several:

> ... the position in the catalog of an editor's name as added entry is the same as it would have been if his name had been used as main entry. Likewise, the position for names of periodicals and newspapers when used as added entries for collections from them will be the same as when they were used as the main entry. Thus, files under a name are kept in tact and the books that are now appearing in our catalogs under title main entries in even greater numbers will be found as readily under the names connected with them as they would have been when those names were the main entries. Those who do not interfile added entries with the main entries may achieve the same arrangement by making the added entry in the form of an author-title double heading, but this is a more cumbersome method. The interfiling of *all* secondary entries in the author file also makes possible the omission of the term *joint* to identify joint authors, joint compilers, etc., in the tracing. A joint author is now traced with no designation ...[68]

The value of the main entry is thus diminished in multiple-entry catalogs since it is disregarded in filing, except for those authors used as main entries.

The special status of the main entry has been further diminished with the introduction of the computer into the cataloging process. It is possible, using an automated catalog, to list bibliographical records under as many identification tags as needed—author, title, date, publisher, etc. Any or all of these tags can be used to retrieve the bibliographic record that is of concern. Thus, again the distinction between main and added entries loses its significance; both headings become merely alternative tags for the same record.[69]

The University of Chicago's *Requirement Study for Future Catalogs* presents this view:

> The introduction into library technology of computerized information handling systems affords opportunities for increasing catalogs' efficiency as finding devices. Automated systems could allow multiple coordinate searching on a number of information fields, or approaches—a procedure which is impractical if not impossible, with alphabetically arranged card catalogs. Thus a library patron desiring to retrieve a particular book might thus be able to interrogate an automated catalog with whatever fragmentary information he could provide.[70]

Present catalogs provide for locating an item only by means of the author or other individuals who share responsibility for the item, including corporate bodies, translators, editors, illustrators, etc.; by means of title of the item or its subject; and, in very few instances, by means of the series of which the item is a part. In an automated catalog, however, the number of access points, or entries, for any given book can then be increased greatly beyond these.

Finally, the *major* reason for the importance attached to the main entry has to do with the assembly of titles under a given author according to the literary unit principle. Cutter, in his *Rules*, suggested that the objectives of the catalog as they concern the author are two:

1. To enable a user to find a book of which the author or the title is known, and
2. To show what the library has by a given author.[71]

These two objectives have been implicit in the various cataloging codes that have followed Cutter's even up to the present day *AACR* 1967. The objectives were rephrased by Lubetzky in his code in 1960,[72] and again were affirmed by the International Conference on Cataloging Principles in 1961.[73]

The first objective is an expression of the finding list function of the catalog, that is, to show whether the library has a particular book known to the inquirer. This has been a stated function of the catalog from as far back as the sixteenth century.[74]

The second objective, that of showing what a library has on a given author, is derived from the literary units principle, that is, the principle of grouping together in one place in the catalog all the works of an author, including as well all editions and translations of his works. This principle seems to have been first formulated by Thomas Hyde of the Bodleian Library.

He makes clear that an author known under several names is to be entered under a single selected form, that translations should be entered under the author of the original work, and that where a pseudonym is used, no pains should be spared to identify the author and at least to make cross-reference from him.[75]

These two objectives are quite often in conflict with one another, because each has different requirements. For the first, "the primary criteria for finding a book are the author and title as these appear on the title-page of the volume itself."[76] Thus, it is possible that different books by the same author will be entered under different forms of entry. It is not unusual that an author uses different names on the title pages of his different books or even different spellings of his name. The second objective, on the other hand, requires that the different works and different editions and translations of the works of an author be brought together. This can be attained either by selecting a single form of entry for each author, or by scattering the books for a single author under different entry forms, with the provision that suitable references, i.e., *see also* references, be made.

The conflict between these two objectives has led to a controversy which has been the subject of several meetings[77] and much published literature.[78] Throughout the history of cataloging the first objective has been given prime consideration inasmuch as the finding list function has always been considered the most important function of the catalog. The second objective, while also considered important, has often been sacrificed to the first. Jewett, for example, is of the opinion that "a catalogue is designed to show what books are contained in a particular collection, and nothing more."[79] Bishop also feels that the catalog is "an instrument whereby" the user can find out "whether the library has a book he wants, or whether it has any books on some topic he is interested in."[80] Bishop goes on to state that the catalog "may be used for other purposes but these two are the prime reason for its existence."[81]

A very recent similar view is that of George Piternick:

It is obvious, however, that the requirements of a mere finding list are simpler than those of a catalog meant to serve the purposes of precise bibliographic identification and establishment of bibliographic relationship. The relative importance of the three functions in libraries is also unquantifiable and dependent upon the nature and use of a given book collection. It may be safe, however, to conclude that the use of a catalog as a finding list is most certainly the most frequent function quantitatively, if not necessarily the most important function.[82]

Quantitatively, use studies confirm what Piternick points out, namely that the reason most users approach the catalog is to find out whether a known item is in the library. Ben-Ami Lipetz, in his study *User Requirements in Identifying Desired Works in a Large Library*, found that 73 percent of his sample of catalog users were searching for a particular known item, while only 6 percent were attempting an author search, that is, attempting to determine all works of a given author, publisher's series, etc., and 16 percent were searching by subject,[83] which might have revealed more titles.

F. H. Ayers *et al.,* in their study of the accuracy of the information users of large scientific special library brought to the catalog, found results similar to those of Lipetz. Out of 450 user requests only one (2.2 percent) contained author information alone and 421 (94 percent) gave both author and title information, which, in effect, specifies a known item. Their study also showed that more books were cited on request forms by title only than by author only. Twenty-eight requests cited only the title.[84]

A more comprehensive study is *Types of Catalog Search and Their Relationship to Some Characteristics of the Users* by Renata Tagliacozzo. The population studied consists of the users of one large university library and the users of a large public library. In the university library out of 2,164 searches, 1,489 (68.8 percent) were for known items and only fifty searches (2.3 percent) were for "any book by author." In the public library the figures were slightly different: out of 517 searches, 256 (49.5 percent) were for known items and only twenty-nine (5.6 percent) were for "any book by author."[85]

The above studies show that the second objective of the catalog, that of assembling literary units, is not of special importance to catalog users; this objective, however, is considered of prime importance by such librarians of stature as Spalding, Lubetzky, Pettee and many others. To accomplish the assembling of literary units the main entry is seen as essential, and it is on these grounds that the main entry is preferred to the title unit entry.[86]

While Sumner Spalding questions the merits of the main entry for listing certain bibliographical entities, he regards the main entry system as generally effective in displaying the intellectual products of each author.[87]

Pettee opposed Hanson in 1936, when she favored the German tradition of entering works of corporate bodies under title. Her basic premise was that "the book in hand is considered not as a single item but as a representation of a literary unit."[88] She later observed that "assembling literary units has come to the front as important, and our term "main entry" recognizes this as a primary function.[89]

Lubetzky can probably be considered the strongest supporter of the main entry and consequently the strongest voice opposing the title unit entry. As to the function of the main entry, he writes that this is

> to represent a publication not as a distinct entity but as an edition of a particular work by a particular author, and so as to relate it to the other editions and translations of the work and to the other works of the author, requires that the main entry should be under the author's name, followed by a title chosen to designate the work . . .[90]

In opposing the title unit entry, Lubetzky advances the idea that the assembling of literary units on a secondary level, that is, subsuming main entries under added entries and subject headings, is equally important, and that the title entry cannot contribute to this assembly.

> For when the main entry is designed to represent a publication as an edition of a particular work by a particular author, the result is that the added entries under the subject and other added headings will similarly be related; but if the basic entry is to be under the title of the publication, the entries under a given subject heading will be indiscriminately arranged alphabetically by the wording of their titles rather than their intrinsic interrelation.[91]

Lubetzky believes the arrangement by main entry under added entries "is a more logical and useful arrangement than the one that would result from entering the works under their titles. . . ."[92] Moreover, he is of the opinion that "this type of organization of the catalog is more satisfactory to its user. . . ."[93]

While philosophically attractive, the belief that literary units can be assembled by means of the main entry is subject to contradictions and cannot be maintained in practice. The writings of some of the proponents of the main entry, as well as our present cataloging rules, provide counter examples to show that the main entry does not always have this function of assembling literary units.

One instance is the case of serial publications. While Lubetzky considers the main author entry essential for assembling literary units, he recommends that serials, with a few exceptions, be entered under their titles. He further recommends that, whenever the title of a serial changes, each title be treated as representing a different serial. This he recommends for the following reasons:

> In the case of a periodical or serial which appears over a long period of time and is subject to various changes of title, it is not to be expected that a writer citing a given volume will inquire what the original title was, or what the relation of the given title is to any other title, and the purposes of the catalog will therefore better be served if each title is entered separately and provided with notes indicating its relation to any other titles.[94]

Similarly, with respect to changing serial titles, Rule 6D1 of the *AACR* states ". . . make a separate entry for the issues appearing after the change."[95] This practice scatters the different issues of a given serial under different entries and thus runs counter to the belief that a function of the main entry is to preserve literary units. In this case literary units are preserved by added entries and by notes which relate titles to each other. One wonders why it is that, although maintaining a single main entry for the sake of the literary units principle is important for monographs that change their titles, this is unimportant for serials that change their titles.

As for Lubetzky's assumption that "it is not to be expected that a writer citing a given volume will inquire what the original title was, or what the relation of the given title is to any other title," it is after all only an assumption. Indeed, we can assume that a writer may not so inquire, but we can equally well assume that he might.

Difficulties in depending on the main entry to preserve literary units arise again in the case of pseudonymous authors. Alternative Rule 42B states:

> If works of an author appear under several pseudonyms or under his real name and one or more pseudonyms, enter each work under the name he used for it. Make *see also* references to connect the names.[96]

Lubetzky approves of this practice of different entries for works that appear under different names of an author. He suggests that if an author

> . . . writes under his real name but also uses a pseudonym in a special literary genre . . . in this case his works should be entered under the names appearing in them, and that an information card should be made to inform the users of the catalog of this fact.[97]

Here, again, the belief that the function of the main entry is to preserve literary units is undermined inasmuch as an author's work will appear in the catalog under more than one form of his name. In this case literary units are preserved by cross references. But the point is that this is not done by the main entry.

Another example of questioning the literary units function of the main entry is provided by the case of works of shared authorship, that is, where there is no principal author and where the authors are more than three. Rule 3B2, which applies to this case, requires a main entry under title and an added entry under the first author only.[98] This rule not only questions the professed function of the main entry, it threatens the literary units principle itself. First, by prescribing main entry under title it undermines the importance of the main author entry in attaining literary units; and second, by requiring an added entry for only one author it results in incomplete literary units. Since only the author first named on the title page will have an entry in the catalog, not all literary units are preserved. Literary units exist for some authors and not for others. As if this were not contradiction enough, Lubetzky recommends that, regardless of the number of authors, all works of shared authorship where a principal author is not indicated be entered under their titles. He feels that the practice of entering a work of two or three authors under the one named first on the title page is an exception which is both "illogical and impractical";[99] entry, he feels, should be made under title. However, he also feels that author entries are needed to preserve literary units. Do not these beliefs contradict each other?

A final illustration, but not the last that could be given, of contradiction to the literary units function of the main entry is the case of corporate bodies which change their name. Rule 68 of *AACR* calls for separate entries under each name. It states:

> If the name of a corporate body has changed (including change from one language to another), establish a new heading under the

> new name for cataloging publications appearing under this name. Make appropriate cross references between the headings under which publications of the body appear in the catalog.[100]

Lubetzky approves of this rule on the grounds that "the works of a corporate body are normally cited and looked for under the names under which they are issued."[101] Since this might be true for corporate authors, is it unreasonable to suppose that this might also be true for personal authors?

Here again, then, in the case of corporate bodies which change their names, literary units are not preserved as a function of the main entry but rather as a function of cross references.

If, in all the illustrations cited above and the many others that can be found, the main entry is not effective in assembling literary units, what then is the function of the main entry? The question can perhaps be clarified by looking particularly at Lubetzky's position regarding the assembly of literary units by main entry under added entries and subject headings.

As stated earlier, Lubetzky claims that bringing together the works of an author under added entries is "more logical and useful." On what evidence does Lubetzky make this claim? It can be argued, for instance, that a title arrangement under a subject heading might be of more interest to the user. A user who is searching under a subject heading usually does not know an author's name. He is interested in materials on the subject rather than in an author on the subject. If the logic of this reasoning is granted, then titles of books are more related to the subjects covered in books than are authors of books. This suggests that a title arrangement would be more useful. Moreover, as was indicated earlier, many libraries do not interfile their added entries and subject headings by the main entry; they file by title. Thus, this claim of logic and usefulness made by Lubetzky is far from proven.

Lubetzky's claim seems to ignore the fact that in many cases main entries are made under the title even when the author or authors are named on the title page. Even Lubetzky himself recommends entering works of shared authorship,[102] works of changing authorship,[103] serials,[104] etc., under their titles. If the arrangement by main entries under added entries is "more logical and useful," is it illogical in these cases?

Finally, with respect to the arrangement by main entry under added entries, it can be pointed out that in many cases the literary units resulting from such an arrangement would be incomplete. In other words, not all the works or publications of a given author would be brought together under a subject heading or under his name as an added entry. For example, in the case of works of shared authorship and where authors are three or fewer, the main entry is usually under the first-named author. Thus, in this case, the literary units assembled under a subject will be only for that author selected as the main entry. No assembly will occur for the other named authors under the same subject. Also it can happen that not all the works of an author will come together under one subject heading. It is very common for one author to write on different subjects—or even if writing on the same subject, he may treat it in different books from different points of view. This results in the scattering of his books under different subject headings or under several subdividions of the same subject heading. It is also not uncommon that some books (such as fiction, poetry, etc.) will have no subject headings.

Incompleteness of literary units assembled under added author entries can occur in several other cases. An example of this is the case of translators or illustrators. Added entries are made for these individuals only if they are "important" or "needed"; or if the translation is "free" or "is in verse." However, literary units will not be complete unless added entries are provided for each one of these individuals.

It should be clear from the above discussion that the assembling of literary units is not a function of the main entry. Actually the achieving of complete literary units requires a combination of several elements: 1) entries for all the authors on the title page of a book, without exception, 2) correct form of heading, and 3) necessary cross references. In other words, to assemble a complete literary unit for an author we must first provide an entry for him, and second, choose one of two things: either select only one form of his name to be used consistently as the entry for all his works and make appropriate *see* references from all other variations of his name; or, enter each of his books under the form of his name listed on the title page and make the necessary *see also* references to relate his different works to one another.

The role of the main entry in assembling literary units is therefore only partial. The main entry is effective in this respect only with books of single authorship; but here, too, the form of heading and the necessary cross references play an important role.

It can be said, then, that the second objective of the catalog—the one relating to the assembly of literary units—is closely dependent upon form of entry. The abandonment of the main entry would not affect this. If we select the right main entry but not the right form of heading, no literary units will be assembled. On the other hand, if we do not select the right main entry, but we provide the necessary added entries and the right forms for these entries, as well as the necessary cross references, the second objective of the catalog will be served.

The above discussion on the topic of the main entry leaves us once more with the same question: What is the function of the main entry? One wonders.

The Title Entry in the West

In the Western world the concept of the title unit entry has not yet been accepted. Although many books have main entries under their titles, title entries have been used only as a last resort and in all cases they are considered only as substitutes for author entries. As we have seen earlier, the Western cataloger has always favored author entries over other entries. This has been a matter of tradition—a tradition which has led to much time and effort being spent establishing author main entries, which is especially time-consuming in those instances where the author does not appear on the title page or in any other place in the book. There is, however, a certain amount of disagreement about author entries among Western catalogers.

40

The German cataloger, for instance, did not accept the corporate author principle and enters works with corporate authors under their titles. The Anglo-American cataloger, on the other hand, is more rigid with regard to the concept of author main entry. He will not enter a book under its title unless he is really not able to find any author entry. In other words, the title entry is used only by default. Pettee makes this clear when she states:

> The author is the first concern of the American cataloger. He searches for anonymous authors. If he is dealing with corporate bodies, he seeks to identify and name the society, institution, or governmental body responsible for the document. If he has an anonymous classic, the search goes back to the source of the classic, and in lieu of author he establishes a form of name under which this literary unit is most correctly known. Only in the case of hopelessly anonymous works of multiple authorship, where personal authors are too many to be serviceable as an entry form, does he resort to title entry.[105]

Many publications cannot be entered under author, either because the author is not given on the title page or because authorship is diffuse. These are the publications that are entered under their titles; they include: 1) anonymous works, 2) serials, 3) sacred scriptures, 4) maps, atlases, motion pictures, etc., 5) works of multiple authorship, and 6) in the German tradition, works of corporate authorship. In the Anglo-American tradition, not only is the title used as a last resort but also, since it is a main entry substituting for an author entry, it can be regarded as an authorship entry. This peculiar idea was advanced by Pettee:

> Perhaps, as a matter of charity, we might stretch the idea of authorship enough to bring these in—the last lambs outside the authorship fold. If the entry under title for these two groups may be considered as substitute for author entry, as I think it may be, all main entries may be considered authorship entries and all come under Cutter's general law: 'Make the author entry under the name of the author, whether personal or corporate, or some substitute for it.'[106]

As indicated earlier, possibly the *major* reason for lack of recognition of the title entry as a unit entry in Western thinking is the mistaken assumption that the main entry should perform an important function, namely to assemble literary units under an author's name. On these grounds, Pettee opposed Hanson when he favored the German tradition of entering works of corporate bodies under their titles. Lubetzky also attacked the title unit entry on the grounds that the main entry under author in modern cataloging practice is "additionally, essential to the second objective—to bring together the works of an author and the editions of a work under all relevant entries: the author, editor, translator, title, subject and any other added entries."[107]

Not only as a unit entry was the title entry given low priority in

Western thinking, but also as an added entry. Even though one of the primary functions of the catalog is to facilitate the location of books of which the author or title is known, title entries are not always made. For many years it has often been the practice of libraries not to make title added entry cards, especially for books whose titles have parallel subject headings and those which begin with common words such as History, Introduction, Journal, Bulletin, etc., to name only a few. Cutter, when he published his rules, seems to have started the practice of only a "more or less" complete title catalog:

> I am regarding the dictionary catalog as consisting of an author catalog, a subject catalog, and a more or less complete title catalog, and a more or less complete form catalog, all interwoven into one alphabetical order.[108]

Since Cutter's rules, this practice has become a convention that has been incorporated in all subsequent rules. For instance, the *AACR* Rule 33P for title added entries states:

> P. Titles. Make a title added entry for every work of known authorship that is published anonymously, and for all other works with the following exceptions:
> 1) Works with common titles that are incomplete or meaning-less without the author's name, such as "Collected Works," "Autobiography," "Letters," "Memoirs," "Bulletin," "Proceed-ings," "Report," etc.;
> 2) Works with long titles that are involved and nondistinctive, unless they are entered under corporate headings or headings that include form subheadings;
> 3) Works with titles that are essentially the same as the main entry heading or a reference to the heading (e.g., Royal Dublin Society; The Royal Dublin Society, 1781 to 1941);
> 4) Works with titles consisting solely of the name of a real person, except when they are works of the imagination;
> 5) Works for which the cataloger has composed a title; and, in a dictionary catalog;
> 6) Works with titles that are identical with a subject heading under which they are entered, if the subject heading as used has no subdivision, or with a see reference that leads directly to such a subject heading.
> Make a title added entry also for any title other than the main title (cover title, partial title, etc.) by which the work is likely to be known.[109]

While Lubetzky recognizes the importance of the title as providing a direct approach to a book (whether or not its author or subject is known), he defends limiting the number of title entries on the grounds that too many title entries increase unnecessarily the size of the catalog and in so doing contribute to the confusion of the user.[110] Margaret Mann comments on the confusion that might be caused by title entries:

> It is often necessary to have title entries for books even though the books have already been entered under their author's name. Titles beginning with a common term, such as "history," "elements," "complete," etc., should seldom find a place in the catalog because they would not be very helpful and because they might be quite numerous.
>
> One difficulty the cataloger has to keep in mind is that readers sometimes mistake a title entry for a subject heading. A reader may think he has exhausted the resources of the library after he has discovered one title card relating to his subject of inquiry.[111]

The reasoning advanced by both Lubetzky and Mann for not making title added entries seems dubious. It can equally well be argued that the confusion of users in using title information in fact results from the lack of title entries in our catalogs.

Actually use studies show that library users are more apt to remember the title than the author of a book, which suggests that the confusion and inconvenience caused the user in using title entries may be the result of inconsistencies and omissions in providing title added entries.

Elizabeth Lamb Tate's investigation gave evidence of the importance of title added entries. She urged "maximum title coverage." And she opposed Lubetzky's criticism of title added entries which is given in his article, "Titles: Fifth Column of the Catalog."

> Many of the partial title added entries that he criticizes are probably unnecessary. But the utility of the title added entry in coping with citations giving incomplete or incorrect author information became readily apparent during this experiment. An added entry for even a non-distinctive title is an aid. The use of subject headings in lieu of title added entries, unless the subject heading can be derived directly and easily from the title of the book, is open to question. Perhaps the reader's confusion between title added entries and subject headings arises, not as Mr. Lubetzky believes, because one duplicates the other, but because the title is not, in the reader's opinion, capitalized correctly in the added entry. Therefore a definition of non-distinctive title that would sharply curtail the number of title added entries excluded on this ground is recommended. In fact, a practical solution that would insure the essential title coverage would be title added entry for each book. Then the vagaries of the catalogers' subjective judgment of titles in terms of distinctiveness would not destroy the integrity of the catalog. An argument in favor of such a policy is the fact that the title added entry is the least expensive of all the secondary entries.[112]

Tate's evidence, which shows that titles are more efficient finding devices than author main entries, was obtained from a citation study. Seventy-eight percent of the citation titles studied matched titles used to the catalog entry, while only 69 percent of the authors matched the authorship element in the catalog entry.[113]

In a survey of three university library catalogs and one public library catalog,[114] training habits of long standing, prior disappointing experience with title added entry coverage, lack of knowledge of filing rules, and ignorance of the user were given as reasons why users tended to overlook the title as the first point of access to a wanted item. The study also showed that the chances that a user would approach the catalog with perfect or nearly perfect information is much higher for title information (70 percent of the cases) than for information about authors (41.9 percent of the cases).[115] It was observed that:

> The larger percentage of 'perfect' titles may be explained by the fact that the meaning of a title usually acts as a built-in corrective mechanism which tends to eliminate minor errors of the orthographic or grammatical type. An equivalent corrective mechanism does not seem to exist for the author.[116]

William Allen Hinkley studied how well users remembered authors and titles of books they had seen. His study showed that only 8.5 percent of the respondents could remember correct author information, while 7.5 percent remembered only correct last names and 5 percent provided incorrect names. The remaining 79 percent gave no response. With the title, however, 19.5 percent of the respondents could remember exact word-for-word titles and 70.1 percent provided titles containing at least descriptive form, that is, a term useful for retrieval. Only 13.8 percent gave wholly useless title information. Matching the titles remembered against the card catalog, 31 percent failed to retrieve the desired items because either title added entries were suppressed in favor of subject headings or the titles were indistinctive.[117] Hinkley observed that it was often the case that "the user has title information and is prevented from using it unless he knows the implications of practical cataloging decisions."[118]

Similarly, F. H. Ayres *et al.*, in describing a survey of the Amsterdam Mechanical Catalog and Research System (AMCOS), reported results that "showed quite conclusively that the title which the user brought to the catalogue was much more likely to be accurate than the author."[119] This survey was conducted to test the comparative accuracy of the information, author versus title, which the library user brings to the catalog. Of the 450 sample requests studied, title information was completely accurate in 90 percent of the cases, while the comparable figure for author information was under 75 percent.[120] Like Tagliacozzo, Ayres attributed the accuracy of title information to the mnemonic features built into titles. "It seems probable that the mnemonic advantages of the title have been underestimated in the past."[121]

The use studies discussed above indicate that in many instances a title entry represents a much more straightforward and sought-after heading than does an author entry. The studies also suggest that users' needs often justify an added entry for every title in our catalogs. This was recognized as early as 1924 by Bishop, who recommended that "the very general habit on the part of readers of recalling titles rather than authors makes the free use of title entries highly advisable."[122]

The free use of title added entries is also advisable from the point of view of the finding-list function of the catalog. The title entry facilitates the retrieval of information, since it is a unique feature of each individual work and thus it distinguishes it from every other bibliographic entry. Having title entries is particularly important since

> it is reasonable to expect many readers to look for a book under the name of its author, or joint author, or editor if it has one, and it is equally reasonable to expect many readers to look under title of a work such as dictionary.[123]

Considering the catalogers' time spent in deciding which titles should have and which should not have added entries, and considering the convenience of the user who is hindered in his research by lack of title entries, it can be asked why should not all books have title added entries. With regard to the question of catalog size, the University of Wisconsin, when it set out to make its title catalog complete by adding the missing entries, increased the size of the catalog by only 18 percent. The original number of title entries in the catalog was 174,199, and 31,643 entries were added.[124] Thus, the missing titles represented only 15 percent of the total number of titles held by the library. With regard to having the large files of cards under words such as "History," "Introduction," etc., this is not new to our catalogs. Already we have many large files under corporate name entries. But these are probably more confusing to the user because of the headings and filing order used than because of the length of the file. In some cases "checking a drawer with a number of similar titles," i.e., nondistinctive, "may for some users be more successful than learning to guess at the proper corporate entry for one title."[125]

Title entries are often not made for books because the title parallels a subject heading. This can cause problems in catalog maintenance as well as problems to the user. Subject headings change as new terminology comes into existence, and the library has to be very alert in going back and making title added entries for books whose subject headings have been changed so that they no longer parallel the titles of the books. This is not an easy job; it is one requiring a considerable amount of time and effort. This practice is also associated with the dictionary catalog, disregarding completely the divided form of the catalog. Of course, any library wishing to convert its catalog to the latter form must perform the time-consuming and costly job of filling in the gaps, as the University of Wisconsin has done.

The practice of not making title entries when subject headings parallel the titles will also cause the user problems. What if the user knows only the title of a book? He cannot find it unless he searches a large number of subject entries. In many cases a single subject heading is represented by several drawers (often more than would be needed for even indiscriminate titles). Thus, the user has to finger hundreds of subject cards to find the item he wants. The search is made even more difficult since the publications are sub-arranged under subject headings by main entry, not by title. Moreover, "it seems doubtful that a user with known title information would transform it into a subject heading and then research, unless he had experience with cataloging rules and practices."[126]

Our discussion of the title *versus* the author approach in searching the catalog has until now been limited to the general user. As we turn to the library staff themselves, we find again that the title approach is frequently favored over the author main entry approach.

With the exception of the reference staff, library staff use of the catalog or any bibliographic tool consists of discovering whether or not the library has a given book, or of finding cataloging information for a book in hand. Thus, as Kilgour explains, "the librarian does not use the author-title entry as a label, but rather as information *per se*."[127]

Searching by the main entry would seem to have many limitations inasmuch as it is a time-consuming process and results in duplication of library materials. "It appears that much time is wasted because the searcher is forced," as Sybil S. Donaldson observes, "to determine main entry before being able to ascertain whether or not the library owns the volume."[128] In an examination of 560 request cards submitted by the faculty of Western Illinois University, it was seen that only 57 percent of the requests were verifiable or could be matched by the main entry as provided by the requestor. The remainder, or 43 percent, required searching under other points of access. A further examination of the same cards showed that only twelve cards (2.5 percent) were incorrect as to title information. The title approach would, therefore, have been successful in 97.5 percent of the cases, compared to only 57 percent of the cases when the main entry approach was used.[129]

The difficulties encountered in searching by main entry result from the fact that the main entry which appears on a request form or is selected by the searcher from the title page of a book may not coincide with the main entry used in the catalog or other bibliographical tool. This could occur for the following reasons:

1. The item in question may be of multiple authorship, of authorship of mixed character, etc. In these cases the searcher is forced to search the item under all the various possible entries. Quite often the searcher is out of luck, for in many instances the information on the request form is incomplete or inaccurate. Also, in many instances, the entry under which the item might be listed in a catalog or a bibliography is selected from some part of the book other than its title page.

2. The author of the item in question may have a personal name subject to variance, as for instance happens in cases of married women, compound names, names with prefixes, titles of nobility and religion, and pseudonyms. All names are subject to variations or

errors in spelling. Furthermore, foreign names in foreign languages are governed by different transliteration techniques. In cases such as these the searcher must look under all possible forms of an author's name—if he knows how!

3. The item in question is by a corporate author. Corporate entries present problems similar in nature to those of personal author entries. The form and/or the spelling of the name of the body in the catalog may vary from the form used on the request form or on the title page of the book.

It can be seen that all of the above difficulties are related to the choice of entry and form of heading. As a consequence the searching process is a problematic and time-consuming task. The searcher quite often has to check under many different entries and/or different forms to be able to locate acquisition information or cataloging information for a given item. This requires a thorough knowledge of rules of entry, form of heading, and filing—a knowledge that is usually possessed only by a professional cataloger. Certainly the requirement is an expensive one, and a painful one in a time when all libraries are concerned about continuous increases in processing costs and decreasing budgets. In many libraries the task of searching is for economic reasons delegated to non-professional staff. Even so, however, it is still a costly operation. Non-professional staff require extensive training to master these rather complex procedures of searching, and this training is expensive, especially considering the high rate of turnover in this level of staff.

Since searching by main entry is a difficult and complex task, it is also time-consuming. The effect of this is a reduction in the productivity of the staff, which in turn increases costs of processing.

The main entry search also affects costs in libraries in another way. Much duplication in the acquisition of library materials can result from uncertainties as to both the main entry and the form of heading. This uncertainty is especially acute when the searching of single entry files is involved (such as in process files, on-order files, etc.). In files such as these, books receive only one entry. If the entry should be an author entry, books by the same author may be scattered through the file under different forms of his name; likewise, books of multiple authorship may be scattered under different entries resulting in a searching problem which will baffle even the initiated searcher.

Another processing area beset by the problems of main entry is the cataloging department. Many libraries use LC cards for their cataloging, yet often these cards cannot be identified because of a problematic main entry. It has been shown that "LC catalog copy has been available, but not used, for 8 to 9 percent of the books cataloged originally in research libraries," and that this lack of utilization is largely due to "the inefficiencies in our present system of file maintenance and bibliographic 'matching'. . . ."[138] The result of this, of course, is unnecessary duplication of effort, which again increases costs of processing.

Unfortunately, there is no literature on how much time or money is wasted on searching and duplication of library materials because of main entry problems. A quantitative analysis of main entry searching seems called for, especially as we will see how searching by title is gaining in popularity.

Rather than its author, the title of a book may be considered its most identifying feature and may be seen to provide the most direct approach for its retrieval. The case of searching permitted by the title contributes to increasing staff efficiency and production, to reducing processing costs, and to eliminating duplicate acquisitions.

Joseph Z. Nitecki observes that:

> Practically, the verification [including searching] of library holdings by title is a simple activity, easily grasped by patrons unversed in library rules, and a fast reliable method in pre-order search by the staff.[131]

Nitecki goes on to argue the value of the title catalog and to explain why title entry is easier and more reliable than author entry. His veiw is very like the views supported by the findings of Tagliacozzo, Hinkley, and Ayres. He states:

> A separate title catalog will be of even greater value to the library staff engaged in checking the library holdings, since the title information on the initial order forms is more often likely to be reliable than the corporate entries in the author catalog.[132]

Probably the most significant indication of the popularity with the library staff of the title approach to searching is the call made upon the Library of Congress by many of the large research libraries receiving depository card sets, as members of the National Program for Acquisitions and Cataloging, that the Library consider arranging these sets by title rather than by main entry. The call became a reality when LC announced in January 1973 that it will begin arranging the sets alphabetically by title abiding to the majority vote. Since this move began in 1969, LC thereupon responded by asking the participants to vote on the issue. It was not until the last study conducted in August 1972, that the majority vote prevailed for the title arrangement. The figures in Table I below, however, show the steady increase and the growth of interest in the title arrangement during these few years since the initial request was made in 1969.

It is interesting to note that some of the libraries that voted for a title arrangement in 1971 "indicated their willingness to contribute money for sharing the cost of having part of the set alphabetized by title in the event that the majority response was again for main entry."[133] LC, however, refused this request on the grounds that it could not provide two different arrangements, and indicated that the request would have to wait until title arrangement received a majority vote.

The above review suggests the coming of a new era in the history of cataloging, exemplified by a wider acceptance of the title entry both as means for the more efficient retrieval of bibliographic information and for the construction of catalogs. It can be asked: How is the profession responding to this change?

TABLE 1
ARRANGEMENT REQUESTED FOR LC CARD SETS*

Arrange-ment Requested	1969		1970		1971		1972	
	No. of Libraries	%	No. of Libraries	%	No. of Libraries	%	No. of Libraries	%
Main Entry	62	73.8	52	59.1	43	51.8	33	43.5
Title	20	23.8	36	40.9	39	47.0	39	51.3
Undecided	2	2.4	—	—	1	1.2	4	5.2
TOTALS	84	100.0	88	100.0	82	100.0	76	100.0

*The figures in this table are compiled from the results of the questionnaires published by LC in the National Program for Acquisitions and Cataloging.

NOTE: Percentages cited in tables are rounded off to the nearest tenth of one percent; therefore they will not always total exactly 100%.

The profession's response is showing itself in several ways. It is now the practice in many libraries to arrange acquisition tools such as in-process and on-order files by title. Other libraries have started to make their title catalogs complete—that is, to provide a title added entry for every single title in their collections.

Examples of such libraries are those of C. W. Post College and the University of Wisconsin—Milwaukee. E. Hugh Behmyer reports that in the catalog of C. W. Post College Library "a title card is made . . . for each and every book in the library." He also adds that "it is the rule of the library that the title used is the exact title of the book and is not a title made up by the cataloger." In the opinion of the library management this is "a matter of accurate bibliographic reporting."[134]

The University of Wisconsin—Milwaukee completed its title catalog in September 1967. As Nitecki explains, "the single most important decision made was the inclusion of at least one card for each title in the collection."[135] This decision was motivated by the desire to provide the library patron with a catalog simple in scope while providing the staff with an efficient tool.

> In the final analysis, the advantages of including all titles outweighed the disadvantages. It was reasoned that the avoidance of exceptions in the coverage of the title catalog would contribute to the simple interpretation of its scope by patrons, while the completeness of the title coverage would significantly increase the reliability of the catalog for searching purposes by the staff.[136]

Another indication of this trend toward complete title catalogs is a study of ten computer-produced book catalogs by George Piternick. Piternick found that title entries were used for all items included in the catalogs, with one exception—the catalog of the Baltimore County Public Library system, "where title entry is provided only when the title is distinctive."[137]

Another response of the profession is in the reflected need, especially of libraries' staff, for simple bibliographic tools to assist in verifying information and in retrieving LC cataloging copy. Title catalogs especially designed to meet this need have appeared. In 1971 the Gale Research Company began its publication, *English Language Books by Title: A Catalog of Library of Congress Cards, 1969-70*, in twenty volumes. This publication will be followed by quarterly and annual supplements to cover cards published by LC from 1971 to the present.

Similarly, Information Dynamics, which publishes the *Micrographic Catalog Retrieval Systems* (the National Union Catalog in microform), began a title index to their catalog in 1970.

Computerized catalogs also have recognized the importance of the title approach. The Ohio College Library Center (OCLC) system provides for the searching of large files of MARC II records by title. According to the designers of the system, the title index was compiled to meet the needs of several of the large research libraries in the system. These libraries had requested such an index because their experience "had shown that the staff could locate entries in files more readily by title than by author and title."[138] An interesting feature of the title approach at OCLC is that it uses a truncated search key "sufficiently specific to operate efficiently as a title index to a file of 135,938 MARC II records."[139] In an experiment conducted by the OCLC staff it was found that a key consisting of the first three characters of the first non-English article word of each title plus the first character of each of the following three words could retrieve a single entry 84 percent of the time and one or more entries, up to five entries, 99.1 percent of the time.[140]

As can be noted, the catalogs we have been discussing represent mostly individual efforts of private publishers or institutions. It is hoped that the Library of Congress will come to assume a leading role in the step forward to the simplification and betterment of bibliographical tools and to the lowering of processing costs.

The final and most significant response of the profession with respect to title entry has been the call in the literature for librarians to adopt the "title unit entry." The last decade has witnessed a strong movement in this direction, especially in the Western world.

To mention only a few authors, el-Mahdi, Wells, Jeffreys, Daily and Myers, and Tait have all advocated the title unit entry and recommended its adoption. These writers, unlike the earlier ones, were motivated not only by a desire for international cooperation and uniformity, but also by a strong conviction that the main entry is unnecessary.

el-Mahdi, in 1961, conducted a comparative study of five codes of cataloging rules based on the main entry with a view to establishing a set of rules for Arabic books. His study revealed many inconsistencies in the codes investigated resulting from the main entry principle. He therefore concluded that:

A basic card which has no heading but includes only the description, and the location (in a subsidiary position), is found to be most convenient in cataloging Arabic books.[141]

The reasons he gives for this conclusion are that in the Arab countries:
1. Libraries may achieve uniformity in one kind of catalog; this is the basic card caralog, or, in other words, the title catalog.
2. For international cooperation, the basic card procedure can aid in achieving unification which UNESCO is working to bring about.
3. Use of the basic card procedure in the Arab libraries will save the expense of recataloging their holdings and revising their catalog cards to conform to some Western code, for, though the card is constructed on a different concept, it will have the same form.
4. The author catalog will contain one kind of entry, that is author entries, and the title catalog will consist of basic cards only.
5. The basic card procedure will allow each library to choose headings for basic cards according to its local code.
6. The procedure suggested for cataloging will help foreign libraries to use catalog cards produced in the Arab countries in their catalogs, requiring only the addition of the appropriate heading in Latin script.[142]

Two years later Tate conducted a study to investigate the effectiveness of the main entry according to both the ALA 1949 rules and Lubetzky's *Code of Cataloging Rules* (CCR). She questioned the validity of the main entry.

> It is tempting at the conclusion of this experiment to examine philosophically the fundamental premises of the American cataloging system and to wonder whether the Oriental approach of the main entry under title may not have merit.[143]

For reasons such as these, Daily and Myers proposed "that we discard the concept of the main entry and that the unit entry in a catalog system be the title entry, with each other required entry simply inserted above the unit entry without altering it."[144] The advantage of this practice, as they explained,

> is that all the inquiry, debate, interpretation, judgment, and conflict concerning the question 'what shall be the main entry?' has been disposed of, for there is no such question to be asked.[145]

A similar view from the other side of the Atlantic was presented by Jeffreys. He asks "would it not be simpler to abandon the two different types of author entries, main and added, in favour of one kind of author entry using alternative headings?" He goes on to describe the alternative headings.

> There is no reason why a cataloger should not continue to say 'all headings are equal, but one is more equal than others': what the

51

alternative heading system does is to remove the main impediments to successful catalogue searching with which this axiom otherwise burdens the catalogue user.[146]

Jeffreys also indicated in his paper that this method of alternative headings, which really is the same as the method of title unit entry, is used in an experimental catalog compiled by the School of Library Studies at the Queen's University of Belfast.[147]

In the United States the title unit entry is presently in use at Stanford University in its undergraduate library catalog, a catalog that is computer-produced. As described by Richard D. Johnson:

> In the Stanford system a new unit record was introduced. The first element of it is the title paragraph. All headings, main or added, are placed directly above it; and if entry under title is desired, a title entry is made in hanging-indention form.
>
> The Stanford catalog thus does away with the main entry concept completely. The necessity, or even wisdom, of setting apart one field in the machine record as main entry may be questioned.[148]

Almost exactly the same position was taken by Tait when he observed that

> if the basic catalogue record for an item were to be regarded as title, imprint and collation, with the appropriate headings added at the top of each entry in the catalogue—author, subject, series, etc., the problem of main entries would disappear and much more flexibility could thus be introduced into the catalogue.[149]

Another strong voice for the title-unit entry is that of Wells, also from Great Britain. During the Brasenose Conference on the Automation of Libraries, he condemned use of the main entry and asked that it be abandoned in favor of the title-unit entry. Motivated by the implications of computer technology, and in particular by the need for a standard format for machine-readable catalog records, he recommended exploring the possibility of a catalog record which dispenses with the main entry heading.[150] Wells regards the main entry as being of little purpose.

> In many ways it would be easier to plan a catalogue record which began with the title, for this would dispense with the notion of a main entry heading—a notion which has occupied more of our time to little purpose than everything else in librarianship except, perhaps, classification and subject indexing. There is little doubt in my mind that we could get international agreement on a standard format for a machine-readable catalogue record if we dispensed with the necessity for a main entry heading. In theory, it would be just as convenient, through the medium of the computer, to recall the whole catalogue record via any search

factor, as it would be to recall part of it or to be referred to some other main entry heading for further search. In these circumstances, the task of planning the input data is reduced to decisions as to the content and format of the catalogue record and the number and form of the factors through which it may be recalled.[151]

Wells expressed a hope that an international committee would set up an international standard for the content of a catalog record and not a new code for headings.[152]

In 1969, Wells' hope was to some extent realized. During the International Meeting of Cataloging Experts held in Copenhagen, an international Working Party on Standard Bibliographic Description was appointed. The Working Party was charged with the responsibility of drafting a set of rules for standardizing the elements of bibliographical descriptions of monographic publications. In the spring of 1971, the Working Party finished its final draft, and the International Standard Bibliographic Description (ISBD) was adopted by the IFLA Committee on Cataloging. Already the *British National Bibliography* and the *Deutsche Bibliographie* are conforming to the Standard. The ALA Descriptive Cataloging Committee has approved the Standard in principle and LC has conformed so far as to agree to make the necessary revisions in Chapter 6 of *AACR*, North American text. LC will begin using ISBD as soon as the revision is approved by the Descriptive Cataloging Committee and the American Library Association.[153]

Although ISBD is a step towards cooperation and international exchange of bibliographical data, it is clear that regarding the question of headings it only partially realizes Wells' hope.

> The primary objective of ISBD is to provide a standard for preparing the descriptive portion of bibliographical entries (including catalog entries) prepared by the national bibliographical and cataloging agencies of all countries. The resulting entries are intended to become definitive national and international records of bibliographical description, records which should serve as a basis for all listings of the work in the country and for the international exchange of bibliographic data as well. It is also designed to facilitate the conversion of this bibliographical information to machine-readable form.
>
> The ISBD establishes the essential elements of bibliographical description and the order and sometimes the form in which the elements should appear. Also designated are certain standard marks of punctuation for the separation of major fields of the description and, in some cases, of elements within these fields. It is concerned with the standardization of the transcription of the title page data, of the collation, and of notes; it is not concerned with the choice and form of heading for a work.[154]

The above statement makes it clear that even with the adoption of ISBD the main entry continues to be a part of our cataloging practice and our cataloging code continues to include rules for its choice.

Hicks and Tillin recently prescribed the title main entry for all nonbook material. It seems fitting to end this historical review of the title unit entry during the 60s with a comment they make concerning its advantages:

> The advantages of title main entry are numerous. The busy librarian who devotes the major portion of her time to working with individuals and groups cannot find the hours necessary for searching out various rules for main entry which differ for each type of material. Nor can she be expected to remember in detail the order of main entry preference for composers, performers, producers and other persons considered important. This is one of the tasks of the professional cataloger, who is at present in short supply and expensive to procure. For the practicing librarian, title main entry establishes simplicity of procedure and standardization. For the user of instructional resources it minimizes frustration since the majority of these materials are requested by title. For future growth of the collection and the possibility of automation in library procedures it provides a set-up that will adapt, without difficulty to computer processing.[155]

Although the movement towards the adoption of the title unit entry concept began to intensify in the sixties, it is evident that this concept, which has always been attributed to the East, has had a long history in the West. Indeed it can be seen from the literature that more has been written about the title unit entry in the Western world than in the countries which adopt it.

Probably Charles C. Jewett is the first notable in the historical development of the title unit entry in its mature form in the Western world. In 1852, he proposed to the Smithsonian Institution the idea of compiling "a general catalog" of books in the United States. His plan was to

> STEREOTYPE THE TITLE SEPARATELY, and to preserve the plate or blocks, in alphabetical order of the title, so as to be able readily to insert additional titles, in their proper places, and then to reprint the whole catalogue.[156]

He felt headings, if they are names, should stand on plates distinct from the title.[157] He also insisted that

> every name, or other word, used as a heading, is to be printed, in the title, in small capitals; thus each stereotyped title will show, at a glance, the heading under which it belongs.[158]

The similarity between Jewett's plan and the description of the title unit entry made by modern writers is very clear. Jewett's plan was ahead of its time; however, it involved technical difficulties that caused it to fail. No one has paid much attention to it or attempted to deal with the technical difficulties. It has been Cutter's rules which have influenced our cataloging practice up until the present time.

The next attempt to promote the title unit entry was not until 1929. In the first world Congress of Librarians and Bibliography held in Rome, Z. Tobolka expressed the need for union catalogs of international scope and a cataloging code of international character. He then suggested that cards produced for international use should contain only the exact transcription of the title (followed by the author statement, imprint, etc.) and that space should be left above the title for the insertion of headings according to local codes.[159] The significance of Tobolka's proposal stems from its being put forward with a view to international cooperation and uniform cataloging. It recognizes for the first time the important role of the title unit entry in achieving these two objectives.

One of the effects of the International Congress and Tobolka's proposal might be an article written in 1935 by James C. M. Hanson entitled "Corporate Authorship Versus Title Entry." In this article, Hanson raised the question of the title *versus* the author entry, especially with respect to publications of corporate bodies. He suggested the use of the title entry on corporate bodies.[160]

Hanson's article was met by opposition from Julia Pettee. In 1936 she wrote an article, "The Development of Authorship Entry and the Formulation of Authorship Rules as Found in the Anglo-American Code,"[161] in defense of the main entry.

With the exception of Hanson's article, no other positive view regarding the "title unit entry" was presented in the literature until the end of the 1940s. The subject was revived again in 1949 by Wilma Radford, who recommended the use of the title entry. She indicated that the idea was also mentioned "by John Metcalfe in notes written by him for the library school in Sydney," and that the practice of entering under title is followed by the library board of New South Wales. The board distributes cards prepared according to this practice to public libraries as a central cataloging service.[162]

A year later Ahlstedt, in his article "Unit Cataloguing," discussed once again and in detail the title unit entry. According to Ahlstedt the catalog entry has three main functions—rubrication, description and location.[163] Rubrication, or the provision of headings for entries, can itself be based on various approaches to the publication cataloged. Ahlstedt feels that rubrication must be the expression of an aspect of the book useful to a reader who wants to find it, not merely a device for arranging entries.[164]

Like Tobolka, both Radford and Ahlstedt put forward their proposals as a means for international cooperation and uniformity in cataloging.

Also of interest during the 1940s was the actual use of the title unit entry practice by Samuel W. Boggs and Dorothy C. Lewis in the cataloging of maps and atlases. In 1945 they published their book, *The Classification and Cataloging of Maps and Atlases*,[165] describing this practice.

Another long period of silence followed the proposals advanced in the late 1940s and the early 1950s, and it was not until the 1960s that the concept of the title unit entry began to see wider acceptance in the Western world.

Summary and Need for the Study

There are two schools of thought with regard to the problem of choice of entry. These are the Western and the Oriental schools. Both schools aim at the construction of catalogs which will fulfill two objectives stated in the Paris Principles:

> The catalog should be an efficient instrument for ascertaining
>
> 2.1 Whether the library contains a particular book specified by
>   (a) Its author and title, or
>   (b) if the author is not named in the book, its title alone, or
>   (c) if author and title are inappropriate or insufficient for identification, a substitute for the title; and
>
> 2.2 (a) which works by a particular author and
>   (b) which editions of a particular work are in the library.[166]

The Oriental and Western schools, however, differ greatly with regard to the means for fulfilling the above objectives. The Western and more popular school advocates the main entry ptinciple, which is based on the determination of authorship responsibility. However, the main entry principle is not really a principle. As Spalding points out, the term principle "is unfortunate because it carries the connotations of truth as opposed to error, of right as opposed to wrong. The 'principles' we have been discussing are more accurately systems of bibliographic listing.[167]

Moreover, the main entry requires for its determination a rather complex set of rules despite which in many cases determinations are based on arbitrary as well as biased decisions. The result is that having to choose a main entry unnecessarily complicates the cataloging process, hinders the identification of bibliographical information, and increases the costs of processing. More important perhaps is the fact that the main entry does not by itself fulfill the objectives of the catalog stated earlier. In particular the assembling of literary units is not a function of the main entry alone.

On the other hand, the Oriental school adopts the title unit entry, an approach which requires only the description of the item in hand and the addition of the author entry or other entries necessary for the identification of the book. This is a rather simple, standard and straightforward approach.

Proponents of the title unit entry, of course, recognize that authors are as important as titles when it is a question of entries or tags for identifying and retrieving items. However, no preference is given to one author over another. Thus, no rules are required for the choice of entry, and no arbitrary decision making is required—the effect of which is to reduce the time and money required for processing. As for fulfilling the second objective of the catalog, that of assembling literary units, the title unit entry relies on added entries only. For this, a set of rules for the form of headings and cross references is required, but this is required in the Western school as well. What the adoption of the title unit entry means is the elimination from our present cataloging rules of a rather sizable number of rules—namely, the first chapter, or the first 32 rules.

Given the evidence favoring the title unit entry, the main entry principle remains an integral part of our cataloging practice. Even the latest attempt toward adopting an International Standard Bibliographic Description could not free itself from this principle. The ISBD published in 1971 by the International Federation of Library Associations states:

> For the majority of alphabetical lists the headings will be determined by codes of rules based on the *Statement of Principles* of the ICCP.[168]

The question arises as to whether we have to make another concession in favor of the main entry, and if so, why? If the main entry continues to be a part of our cataloging practice, will our cataloging code be characterized by a number of complicated and unnecessary rules?

Whenever cataloging rules have been revised, no attempt has been made to analyze these rules in light of the validity of the main entry. While there have been many who have advocated dispensing with the main entry and adopting the title unit entry, no in-depth analytical study has yet been made to examine critically the main entry as a basis for the construction of cataloging rules. It is the purpose of the present study to examine systematically the main entry as adopted by the *AACR*. If the main entry is essential and readily selected, it can be argued that title unit entry is the more elaborate method and main entry will conserve time by omitting unnecessary entries. This is true, however, only if main entry follows necessarily from a given set of decisions, so that, having determined the character of the work at hand, a cataloger is led to one, and only one, choice for main entry. Where subjective judgments arise from two or more equally valid choices, standardization of entry occurs by chance rather than by design.

FOOTNOTES

[1] *The Prussian Instructions; Rules for the Alphabetical Catalogs of the Prussian Libraries*, trans. from 2d ed., 1908, with an introduction and notes by Andrew D. Osborn (Ann Arbor: University of Michigan, 1938).

[2] Charles Coffin Jewett, *Smithsonian Report on the Construction of Catalogues of Libraries, and their Publication by Means of Separate, Stereotyped Titles* (2d ed., Washington, D.C.: Smithsonian Institution, 1853), p. 18.

[3] Seymour Lubetzky, *Principles of Cataloging, Final Report, Phase I: Descriptive Cataloging* (Los Angeles: Institute of Library Research, University of California, 1969), p. 1.

[4] J.C.M. Hanson, *A Comparative Study of Cataloging Rules Based on the Anglo American Code of 1908* (Chicago: University of Chicago Press, 1939).

[5] Valter Ahlstedt, "Unit Cataloging," *Libri*, I, No. 2 (1950), 115.

[6] Eugene R. Hanson and Jay E. Daily, "Catalogs and Cataloging," *Encyclopedia of Library and Information Science* (New York: Marcel Dekker, 1970), IV, 298-300.

[7] Ahlstedt, *op. cit.*, p. 115.

[8] Ruth French Strout, "The Development of the Catalog and Cataloging Codes," *Library Quarterly*, XXVI (October 1956), 254-75; Hanson and Daily, *op. cit.*; Lubetzky, *op. cit.*; Julia Pettee, "The Development of Authorship Entry and the Formulation of Authorship Rules as Found in the Anglo-American Code," *Library Quarterly*, VI (July 1936), 270-90.

[9] Daily, "Binder's Title," *op. cit.*, p. 485.

[10] Ahlstedt, *op. cit.*; Muhammed el-Mahdi, "The Choice of Entry of Books; a Comparative Study of Principles and Rules Which Govern It, with Special Attention to Some Problems Concerning the Entry of Arabic Books" (unpublished master's thesis, Cairo University, Faculty of Arts, 1971)

[11] A. E. Jeffreys, "Alternative Headings," *Catalogue & Index*, No. 8 (October 1967), 4.

[12] Warren B. Hicks and Alma M. Tillin, *Developing Multi-Media Libraries* (New York: R. R. Bowker, 1970), p. 72.

[13] el-Mahdi, *op. cit.*, p. 10.

[14] *Ibid.*, p. 208.

[15] Jeffreys, *op. cit.*, p. 5.

[16] Wilma Radford, "Catalogs, Codes and Bibliographic Control," *College & Research Libraries*, X (October 1949), 396.

[17] *Ibid.*, p. 398.

[18] Strout, *op. cit.*, p. 257.

[19] el-Mahdi, *op. cit.*, pp. 36-44.

[20] Mahmoud el-Sheniti, "Cataloging and Classification of Arabic Books, Some Basic Considerations," *UNESCO Bulletin for Libraries*, XIV (May-June 1960), 105; F. L. Kent and F. Abu Haidar, "Library Development in the Arab World," *Revue Internationale de la Documentation*, XXIX (February 1962), 4.

[21] el-Sheniti, *op. cit.*, p. 105.

[22] el-Mahdi, *op. cit.*, p. 200.

[23] *Ibid.*, p. 201.

[24] Kent and Abu Haidar, *op. cit.*, p. 4

[25] Mahmoud el-Sheniti, *Entries of Arabic Authors, First List up to 1215 H/1800 A.D.* (Cairo: Egyptian Association of Archives and Libraries, 1961).

[26] el-Mahdi, *op. cit.*, p. 239.

[27] Strout, *op. cit.*, p. 257.

[28] Tait, *op. cit.*, p. 17. *Cf.* Andrew Maunsell, *Catalogue of English Printed Books* (London: A. Maunsell, 1595).

[29] *Catalog Rules: Author and Title Entries*, comp. by committees of the American Library Association and the (British) Library Association

(American ed., Chicago: ALA, Publishing Board, 1908), p. 1. Hereafter referred to as AA 1908.

[30]Charles A. Cutter, *Rules for a Dictionary Catalogue* (4th ed., Washington, D.C.: Government Printing Office, 1904), p. 21.

[31]AA 1908, *op. cit.*, p. xv.

[32]*ALA Cataloging Rules for Author and Title Entries*, prepared by Division of Cataloging and Classification, American Library Association, and ed. by Clara Beetle (2d ed., Chicago: American Library Association, 1949), p. 232. Hereafter referred to as ALA 1949.

[33]*Anglo-American Cataloging Rules*, prepared by the American Library Association, *et. al.* (North American text, Chicago: American Library Association, 1967), p. 345. Hereafter referred to as *AACR*.

[34]Margaret Mann, *Introduction to Cataloging and the Classification of Books* (2d ed., Chicago: American Library Association, 1943), p. 114.

[35]Maurice F. Tauber, *et al.*, *Technical Services in Libraries: Acquisitions, Cataloging, Classification, Binding, Photographic Reproduction, and Circulation Operations* (New York: Columbia University Press, 1953), p. 132.

[36]Bohdan S. Wynar, *Introduction to Cataloging and Classification* (4th rev. ed., Littleton, Colo: Libraries Unlimited, Inc., 1972), p. 17.

[37]A. J. Wells, "The British National Bibliography," in *The Brasenose Conference on the Automation of Libraries; Proceedings of the Anglo-American Conference on the Mechanization of Library Services Held at Oxford Under the Chairmanship of Sir Frank Francis and Sponsored by the Old Dominion Foundation of New York, 30 June—3 July 1966*, ed. by John Harrison and Peter Laslett (London: Mansell, 1967), p. 25.

[38]Tait, *op. cit.*, p. 145.

[39]Jay E. Daily and Mildred Myers with the assistance of George M. Sinkankas, *Cataloging for Library Technical Assistants* (Washington, D.C.: Communication Service Corporation, 1969), p. 39.

[40]Henry A. Sharp, "Cataloging: Some New Approaches; What Price the Main Entry?" *Library World*, LVII (January 1956), 116.

[41]*Ibid.*

[42]Pettee, *op. cit.*, p. 273.

[43]Paul S. Dunkin, *Cataloging U.S.A.* (Chicago: American Library Association, 1969), p. 45.

[44]*Ibid.*, p. 8.

[45]Andrew D. Osborn, "Relation Between Cataloguing Principles and Principles Applicable to Other Forms of Bibliographical Work," in International Conference on Cataloguing Principles, Paris, October 8—18th, 1961, *Report* (London: Organizing Committee of the International Conference on Cataloguing Principles, National Central Library, 1963), p. 135. Hereafter referred to as ICCP, *Report*.

[46]Joan Friedman and Alan Jeffreys, "Cataloguing and Classification in British University Libraries: A Survey of Practices and Procedures," *Journal of Documentation*, XXIII (September 1967), 243.

[47]*AACR* p. 2.

[48]Mortimer Taube, "The Cataloging of Publications of Corporate

Authors," *Library Quarterly*, XX (January 1950), 3.

[49] Richard W. Bird and Michael Gorman, "Standards for Standards," *Catalogue & Index*, No. 6 (April 1967), p. 4.

[50] *American National Standard for Title Leaves of a Book* (New York: American National Standards Institute, 1971), p. 3.

[51] *Ibid.*, pp. 7-8.

[52] Frederick G. Kilgour, "Concept of an On-line Computerized Library Catalog," *Journal of Library Automation*, III (March 1970), pp. 6-8; Bernard I. Palmer, "A Time for Theory," *Catalogue & Index*, No. 6 (July 1967), 4.

[53] RECON Working Task Force, *Conversion of Retrospective Catalog Records to Machine-readable Form; a Study of the Feasibility of a National Bibliographic Service*, ed. by John C. Rather (Washington, D.C.: Library of Congress, 1969), pp. 52-53.

[54] Seymour Lubetzky, *Cataloging Rules and Principles; a Critique of the ALA Rules for Entry and a Proposed Design for Their Revision* (Washington, D.C.: Processing Department, Library of Congress, 1953).

[55] Joseph R. Edelen, *Catalog Card Reproduction Project* (Vermillion, S.D.: I. D. Weeks Library, University of South Dakota, 1971), p. 3.

[56] Lubetzky, *Principles of Cataloging*, p. 36.

[57] *Ibid.*

[58] *Ibid.*, p. 28.

[59] Mann, *op. cit.*, pp. 119-20.

[60] Daily, Myers and Sinkankas, *op. cit.*, p. 36.

[61] Dunkin, *op. cit.*, pp. 2-3.

[62] William Warner Bishop, *Practical Handbook of Modern Library Cataloging* (2d ed., Baltimore: Williams & Wilkins Co., 1924), p. 16.

[63] U.S. Library of Congress, *Report of the Librarian of Congress, for the Fiscal Year Ending June 30, 1901* (Washington, D.C.: Government Printing Office, 1901).

[64] Mann, *op. cit.*, p. 105.

[65] Eva Verona, "The Function of the Main Entry in the Alphabetical Catalogue—a Second Approach" in ICCP, *Report*, p. 145.

[66] John J. Boll, Peggy O'N. Parry, and Richard D. Walker, *Introduction to Cataloging* (preliminary ed., Madison, Wis.: Library School, University of Wisconsin, 1966), II, NC-10.

[67] *ALA Rules for Filing Catalog Cards*, prepared by the American Library Association Editorial Committee's Subcommittee on the ALA rules for Filing Catalog Cards, ed. by Pauline A. Seely (2d ed., Chicago: American Library Association, 1968), p. 115.

[68] Pauline A. Seely, "ALA to AA, an Obstacle Race," *Library Resources & Technical Services*, XIII (Winter 1969), 17.

[69] Tait, *op. cit.*, pp. 140-41.

[70] *Requirements Study for Future Catalogs, Progress Report No. 2* (Chicago: Graduate Library School, University of Chicago, 1968), p. 2.

[71] Cutter, *op. cit.*, p. 12.

[72] Seymour Lubetzky, *Code of Cataloging Rules: Author and Title*

Entry; an Unfinished Draft for a New Edition of Cataloging Rules Prepared for the Catalog Code Revision Committee, with an Explanatory Commentary by Paul Dunkin (Chicago: American Library Association, 1960).

[73] ICCP, *Report*.

[74] Tait, *op. cit.*, p. 17.

[75] Pettee, *op. cit.*, pp. 278-79.

[76] Wyllis E. Wright, "General Philosophy and Structure of the Code," in Institute on Cataloging Code Revision, Stanford University, July 9–12, 1958, *Working Papers*, sponsored by the Cataloging and Classification Section of the Resources and Technical Services Division, American Library Association and the Stanford University Libraries (Stanford, Calif.: 1958), p. I-2.

[77] ICCP, *Report, op. cit.*; "Institute on Catalog Code Revision: A Composite Report," *Library Resources & Technical Services*, III (Spring 1959), 123-40.

[78] Lubetzky, *Principles of Cataloging*.

[79] Jewett, *op. cit.*, p. 10.

[80] William Warner Bishop, "Cataloging as an Asset," in his *The Backs of Books and Other Essays in Librarianship* (Baltimore: Williams & Wilkins, 1926), p. 132.

[81] *Ibid.*

[82] George Piternick, "The Machine and Cataloging," in *Advances in Librarianship*, ed. by Melvin J. Voigt (New York: Academic Press, 1970), p. 4.

[83] Ben-Ami Lipetz, *User Requirements in Identifying Desired Works in a Large Library* (New Haven, Conn.: Yale University Library, 1970), p. 2.

[84] F. H. Ayers, *et al.*, "Author versus Title: A Comparative Survey of the Accuracy of the Information which the User Brings to the Library Catalogue," *Journal of Documentation*, XXIV (December 1968), 270.

[85] Renata Tagliacozzo, "Types of Catalog Search and Their Relationship to Some Characteristics of the User," in *Integrative Mechanisms in Literature Growth*, ed. by Manfred Kochen, Report to the National Science Foundation, Vol. 2, Pt. IV (University of Michigan, Mental Health Institute, 1970), p. 29.

[86] Pettee, *op. cit.*

[87] C. Sumner Spalding, "Main Entry: Principles and Counterprinciples," *Library Resources & Technical Services*, XI (Fall 1967), 391-92.

[88] Pettee, *op. cit.*, p. 270.

[89] *Ibid.*, p. 285.

[90] Lubetzky, *Principles of Cataloging*, p. 23.

[91] *Ibid.*, p. 106.

[92] Lubetzky, *Cataloging Rules and Principles*, p. 43.

[93] *Ibid.*, p. 59.

[94] *Ibid.*, p. 47.

[95] *AACR*, p. 22.

[96] *Ibid.*, pp. 74-75.

[97] Lubetzky, *Cataloging Rules and Principles*, p. 46.

[98] *AACR*, p. 16.

[99] Lubetzky, *Principles of Cataloging*, p. 36.

[100] *AACR*, p. 114.

[101] Lubetzky, *Cataloging Rules and Principles*, p. 50.

[102] Lubetzky, *Principles of Cataloging*, p. 36.

[103] *Ibid.*, p. 38.

[104] Lubetzky, *Code of Cataloging Rules*, p. 80.

[105] Pettee, *op. cit.*, p. 270.

[106] *Ibid.*, p. 286.

[107] Lubetzky, *Principles of Cataloging*, p. 34.

[108] Cutter, *op. cit.*, p. 15.

[109] *AACR*, p. 72.

[110] Seymour Lubetzky, "Titles: Fifth Column of the Catalog," *Library Quarterly*, XI (October 1941), 412-30.

[111] Mann, *op. cit.*, p. 128.

[112] Elizabeth Lamb Tate, "Effective Main Entries: A Comparison of the ALA Cataloging Code with Seymour Lubetzky's Draft Revision in Relation to Bibliographic Citations" (unpublished Ph.D. dissertation, University of Chicago Graduate Library School, 1965), pp. 153-54.

[113] *Ibid.*, p. 144.

[114] Renata Tagliacozzo, Lawrence Rosenberg, and Manfred Kochen, "Access and Recognition: From Users' Data to Catalogue Entries," *Journal of Documentation*, XXVI (September 1970), 244.

[115] *Ibid.*

[116] *Ibid.*, p. 240.

[117] W. A. Hinkley, "On Searching Catalogs and Indexes with Inexact Title Information" (unpublished M.A. thesis, University of Chicago Graduate Library School, 1968), pp. 41-42.

[118] *Ibid.*, p. 42.

[119] Ayres, *et al.*, *op. cit.*, p. 271.

[120] *Ibid.*, pp. 266-68.

[121] *Ibid.*, p. 268.

[122] Bishop, *Practical Handbook of Modern Library Cataloging*, p. 107.

[123] Boll, Parry and Walker, *op. cit.*, p. C-29.

[124] Joseph Z. Nitecki, "The Title Catalog: A Third Dimension," *College & Research Libraries*, XXIX (September 1968), 436.

[125] *Ibid.*, p. 432.

[126] Edelen, *op. cit.*, p. 17.

[127] Frederick G. Kilgour, *op. cit.*, p. 4.

[128] Sybil S. Donaldson, "An Investigation of Main Entry Approach for Search of Request Cards" (paper presented to 350 Seminar in Technical Services, University of Pittsburgh, Graduate School of Library and Information Sciences, 1969), p. 16 (typewritten).

[129] *Ibid.*

[130] James E. Skipper, "Future Implications of Title IIC, Higher Education Act of 1965," *Library Resources & Technical Services*, XI (Winter 1967), 47.

[131] Nitecki, "The Title Catalog," p. 431.

[132] *Ibid.*, p. 432.

[133] U.S. Library of Congress. Processing Department. National Program for Acquisitions and Cataloging, *Progress Report*, No. 12 (June 9, 1971), p. 1.

[134] Hugh E. Behymer, "Four-way Catalog," *Library Journal*, XCIII (March 15, 1968), 1083.

[135] Nitecki, "The Title Catalog," p. 432.

[136] *Ibid.*, p. 433.

[137] Piternick, *op. cit.*, p. 13.

[138] Philip L. Long and Frederick G. Kilgour, "A Truncated Search Key Title Index," *Journal of Library Automation*, V (March 1972), 17.

[139] *Ibid.*, p. 19.

[140] *Ibid.*, pp. 18-19.

[141] el-Mahdi, *op. cit.*, p. 8.

[142] el-Mahdi, *op. cit.*, pp. 8-9.

[143] Tate, *op. cit.*, p. 150.

[144] Daily, Myers and Sinkankas, *op. cit.*, p. 40.

[145] *Ibid.*, p. 41.

[146] Jeffreys, *op. cit.*, p. 5.

[147] *Ibid.*

[148] Richard D. Johnson, "A Book Catalog at Stanford," *Journal of Library Automation*, I (March 1968), 21.

[149] Tait, *op. cit.*, p. 143.

[150] Wells, *op. cit.*, pp. 24-32.

[151] *Ibid.*, pp. 24-25.

[152] *Ibid.*, p. 30.

[153] "International Standard Bibliographic Description," in U.S. Library of Congress Processing Department. *Cataloging Information Bulletin*, No. 104 (May 1972), 8-9.

[154] *Ibid.*

[155] Hicks and Tillin, *op. cit.*, p. 173.

[156] Jewett, *op. cit.*, p. 5.

[157] *Ibid.*, p. 23.

[158] *Ibid.*

[159] Z. Tobolka, "Projet d'un code internationale de règles catalographiques," *Atti*, II, p. 121-52.

[160] J.C.M. Hanson, "Corporate Authorship versus Title Entry," *Library Quarterly*, V (October 1935), 457-66.

[161] Pettee, *op. cit.*, p. 270.

[162] Radford, *op. cit.*, p. 397.

[163] Ahlstedt, *op. cit.*, p. 132.

[164] *Ibid.*

[165] Samuel W. Boggs and Dorothy C. Lewis, *The Classification of Maps and Atlases* (New York: Special Libraries Association, 1945).

[166] ICCP, *Report*, p. 26.

[167] Spalding, *op. cit.*, p. 395.

[168] *International Standard Bibliographic Description (for Single Volume and Multi-volume Monographic Publications)*, recommended by the Working Group on the International Standard Bibliographic Description set up at the International Meeting of the Cataloguing Experts, Copenhagen, 1969 (London: IFLA Committee on Cataloguing, 1971), p. IV.

CHAPTER III

THE ANALYSIS:
MAIN ENTRY IN RELATION TO
THE ANGLO-AMERICAN CATALOGING RULES, 1967

The length and complexity of the 1949 *ALA Cataloging Rules for Author and Title Entries* caused dismay in the profession from the time they were published. Critics called for a reevaluation of the basic principles, a systematization, and a simplification of the rules. Seymour Lubetzky's critique, "Cataloging Rules and Principles, 1953," stimulated the demand on both sides of the Atlantic for a new code, more logical and simpler in nature.

During the same decade, there was dissatisfaction with existing cataloging codes in other countries. Revision of cataloging rules were in progress in France, Italy, and the Soviet Union. In Germany the *Prussian Instructions* were under study and investigation was begun with a view to revision.[1] Besides this interest in revision there was a growing interest in cataloging principles, stimulated by the International Conference on Cataloging Principles (ICCP) held in Paris in 1961 and sponsored by the International Federation of Library Associations with a subsidy from UNESCO.[2] The outcome of the conference was a document entitled *Statement of Principles*, hereafter called the *Paris Principles*, which claimed to present the most modern thinking in cataloging theory. In general the *Paris Principles* are open to different interpretations; however, they have not attracted much comment or criticism.

In 1967 the long-awaited *Anglo-American Cataloging Rules*, purporting to adopt the *Paris Principles* (with exceptions), was published on both sides of the Atlantic. Like the AA 1908 Code, the *AACR* was published in two editions, American and British, different in format and text. This difference in format and text subjected the code to criticism by Andrew D. Osborn[3] and others.

The *AACR* differs from earlier codes in that it combines in one volume the rules for entry and headings, description, and non-book materials. Part I covers Entry, Headings for persons, Headings for corporate bodies, Uniform titles, and References. Part II covers Description in four chapters: Monographs, Serials, Incunabula and Photolithographic and other reproductions; Part III covers Entry and description of non-book materials: Manuscripts, Maps, Atlases, Motion pictures, Filmstrips, Music, Phonorecords and Pictures.

Part III deals with both the choice of entry and the description of these materials, but in a prefatory note it is stated that the rules in Parts I and II apply to Part III "to the extent that they are pertinent and unless they are specifically contravened or modified by the rules in the following chapters."[4] The separation of the choice of entry from the choice of the form of heading represents a new feature in the Code. The Code thus recognizes that these are two separate problems. Like its predecessors, the Code is designed primarily for large research libraries. "These rules have been drawn up primarily to respond to the needs of general research libraries."[5] The needs of non-research libraries are, however, met by providing alternative rules where these needs differ from those of the large research library.[6]

Shortly after it was published, the *AACR*, like its predecessors, was subjected to much criticism in that it deviated from the *Paris Principles* and that it was based on tradition rather than principles. It was also criticized for its complexity, which showed a disregard for the new technology and possible computer applications. Some of the criticism suggested simplification of the rules or abridged editions;[7] other criticism asked for complete revision.[8] As a matter of fact, the rules have been under continuous revision and change since their publication. Amendments to the rules were issued by the Library of Congress in its *Cataloging Information Bulletin* and by the Library Association in its *Catalogue & Index*. Still more changes are being proposed by the Library of Congress. "These proposed changes fall into two categories, rewordings of rules to make their intent clearer, and changes to rules which have caused practical problems in application in the Library of Congress catalogue."[9] This continuous revision has caused the British Cataloguing Rules Sub-Committee to indicate under the title "Danger—Code Erosion," that it is "'somewhat worried' by the large number of additions and changes that have already been accepted for the North-American Text, in view of the relatively short operational life of the AACR."[10] The American, or rather the LC, position regarding these revisions was explained by P. R. Lewis and J. C. Downing, who attended the ALA 1969 conference in Atlantic City. They point out that:

> LC tends to take the view, as expressed in the meeting and manifested in the number and range of its amendment proposals since 1967, that this Code is basically a 'preliminary' edition, to be shaped into a final version for later publication.[11]

As has been mentioned, there were four main criticisms of the *AACR*: 1) it deviates from the *Paris Principles*, 2) it does not consider possible computer applications, 3) its rules are complex and difficult to interpret and 4) it is based on tradition rather than principles.

Both the British and American texts deviate from the *Paris Principles*, the British text being the more faithful of the two. The American text makes several exceptions, the result of a Library of Congress conducted study of the theoretical merits of the principles. Certain changes were recommended which were supported by the Association of Research Libraries. These exceptions were regrettable, especially "since those principles were largely an

American product"; since they owe much to the work of Seymour Lubetzky; and since "the Americans voted for their acceptance."[12]

Several reasons were suggested for the departure from the *Paris Principles*. "One ... keeping a little closer to the older traditions of the English-speaking world; the other, that a number of continental libraries felt that the Paris Principles, as a whole, were biased in the Anglo-American direction."[13] Another reason was economical, since certain of the provisions of the *Paris Principles* could result in heavy cost if applied to the great number of entries involved, especially in large research libraries.[14]

Although its revision paralleled the development of modern technology, the *AACR* did not concern itself with the computer and ignored the predictions, happenings, and recommendations put forward during the sixties. During the ICCP, in 1961, C. D. Gull expressed the need for a different definition of cataloging and brought out the fact that machines would bring about a need for modifications in the cataloging rules.[15] Ralph Parker presented a similar view in 1964.[16] The period of the revision of the rules also witnessed the introduction of the MARC project (1966). The Code thus became out of date as soon as, or perhaps even before, it was published. In a colloquium on the *Anglo-American Cataloging Rules*, held at the School of Library Science, University of Toronto, on March 31 and April 1, 1967, Andrew D. Osborn, talking about the effect of automation on cataloging, said that "the 1967 code should have appeared in 1949 and in 1967 we should have had the kind of code that would have pointed the way into the future."[17] More than a year later he indicated that "today we need a specially devised code for computer-based library catalogs."[18] A similar and even more positive view was expressed in 1968 by Theodore Hines who went so far as to recommend the immediate revising of *AACR*.[19] Concern over the impact of computer techniques on cataloging practice led to the IFLA International Meeting of Cataloging Experts held in Copenhagen in 1969. One of the decisions reached in this meeting was that there should be an international standard for bibliographic description for any publication to serve as a means for the international exchange of information.

The new Code, as was mentioned, is complex. "The result of fifteen years labor on the part of the cataloging profession has not been a shorter or simpler code."[20] The *AACR* incorporates 126 rules for entry and form of headings containing some 500 provisions, compared to 158 rules including some 500 provisions in the ALA 1949 Code.[21] It is also evident that the rules as they stand are open to individual interpretations which result in inconsistent decisions.

> The more complex the code (and whatever else one says about the new Anglo-American Rules, they are still rather complex), the greater the variety of different interpretations of it that are to be found in different libraries; and the problem at the centre of a national system—of deciding whether all these different records are really for the same book—may be quite severe.[22]

Since the Code was published, several conferences, symposiums, workshops, etc., have been held to explain and interpret the rules for members of the profession. The proceedings of some of these activities, such as those held at the University of Nottingham in 1967,[23] the University of British Columbia in 1967,[24] the University of Toronto in 1967,[25] and Kansas City in 1968,[26] were published, showing the multiplicity of interpretations of the rules. Individual studies, such as that by Michael Gorman entitled *Study of the Rules of Entry and Heading in the Anglo American Cataloging Rules, 1967 (British text)*, were published by the Library Association of London in 1968. P. R. Lewis and G. E. Hamilton reported that

> there has been a great deal of discussion at meetings of the Cataloguing Rules Committee [of the Library Association] and elsewhere on the subject of the need for an abridged or simplified version of the Anglo-American Cataloguing Rules 1967. One of the most frequent criticisms of the Rules is that they are over long and over complicated.[27]

The fourth main criticism of the Code is that it is based on tradition rather than principles. The rules are little more than a restatement of earlier practices, culminating from the Anglo-American cataloging tradition that began with Panizzi and continued through Cutter, ALA and LA committees and Seymour Lubetzky. As was pointed out earlier, the *AACR* adopted the *Paris Principles*, but with some exceptions. A. H. Chaplin, who wrote the original draft of these principles, states

> ... it was not, as I think I can safely say, a statement of principles of catalogue construction at all, it was rather a set of general rules blending various traditions and designed to provide a basis for intellectual uniformity in cataloging.[28]

Similarly, Raganathan points out that "cataloguing codes till now based on the practice of the last few centuries should be sealed. A new catalogue code should be framed, suited to the cataloguing of the books of tomorrow, and to the needs of 'service libraries'."[29] As a summary of criticism of the *AACR*, Nitecki's description seems appropriate: "The rules therefore are neither purely 'international' or 'modern,' nor are they strictly based upon principles. They are at their best well edited, typographically improved, and pleasantly compiled traditional cataloging rules."[30]

Underlying all these criticisms is the *main entry principle*. The *AACR* still adheres to the authorship principle which insists on the main entry heading under author, a principle which was developed in the sixteenth century. And thus,

> the choice of entry has been treated as a problem of determination of authorship responsibility. Hence the general rules of entry are framed around an analysis of the various patterns in which this responsibility may be distributed between persons, between corporate bodies, and between persons *and* corporate bodies, in the publications that must be cataloged.[31]

Although the Code is designed for the construction of multiple-entry catalogs, it still distinguishes between main and added entries. The first chapter of the *AACR* is devoted to the choice of main and added entries. The rules in this chapter are primarily for determining the main entry of a work. "Enter under" is to be interpreted as "make main entry under...."[32] Rule 33 at the end of this chapter deals with the conditions under which added entries are to be made in addition to those given in the particular rules. This chapter does not, however, contain any major changes or surprises in the sense that application of the new rules will result in substantial difference of entry in catalogs compiled according to the 1949 rules. The basic difference between the two codes is more a matter of layout and arrangement. The new Code brings together a quantity of separate and diffuse rules into a smaller number of logically grouped categories of rules in terms of types of authorship. However, as will be shown later, the adherence of *AACR* to the principle of intellectual responsibility as the main determinant of author heading does not always do what is intended—for instance, in showing patterns of authorship.

The application of the main entry principle results in entries under headings which would be extremely difficult for the uninitiated to find in the catalog, even having the work in hand. When, as it sometimes does, the *AACR* deems the intellectual responsibility concept to be unworkable, it falls back on other concepts, such as the name most permanently or prominently associated with a work, or the concepts of subordinate work and form entry.

The main entry and the distinction between main and added entries seem to be the cause for continuous criticism and revision of the cataloging rules. John Friedman and A. Jeffreys stated that

> ... The new Anglo-American Rules, ... retain unquestioned the concepts of 'main' and 'added' entries. Since cataloguers are themselves often unable to agree on the particular bibliographical tag to be chosen as 'main entry', can we really expect that users, unversed in the mystiques of cataloguing codes, will always concur with whatever is finally chosen? Would it not be more realistic to choose the title as the common bibliographic factor? Libraries would then make as many 'added' entries as they pleased, including one for the 'main' author. We look forward to an early reconsideration of this problem.[33]

A similar view was expressed by Ayers and his collaborators:

> The new A-A *Code* asserts that the principle is firmly established in modern cataloguing and bibliography that a work should be identified by its author and title. Although this is true, it is difficult to find valid reasons for the author rather than the title being accepted as the base for the catalogue, and in fact there are signs that this is now being challenged.[34]

Today, as two decades ago, there are many discussions and studies in the field of cataloging rules, stimulated by the complexity and inconsistency of the *Anglo-American Cataloging Rules, 1967*, by the emergence of computer applications in cataloging operations, and by the need for better methods for bibliographic control. As was mentioned, the *AACR* 1967, currently in use, is constructed around the principle of main entry under author and still distinguishes main entries from added entries. The purpose of this is to provide for a multiple-entry catalog that will enable a user to find a book of which the author or the title is known, show what works a library has by a given author, and what editions the library has of a given work. If these are functions of the catalog, the rules of cataloging should allow objective decision-making to consistently provide the entries that can accomplish these stated functions of the catalog.

In consideration of the criticisms of the *AACR* and in particular of the main entry principle, it is possible to state that the *rules* for the choice of entry in the *Anglo-American Cataloging Rules, 1967*, based on the determination of authorship *principle*, fail to provide an *objective* means for determining the entry that will preserve the stated functions of the catalog.

The dictionary defines *rule* as a regulation governing conduct, action, procedure, arrangement, etc. A rule, usually something adopted or enacted, is often the specific application of a principle. *Principle*, on the other hand, is defined as a fundamental, primary, or general truth on which other truths depend. The dictionary describes *objective* as an adjective used to show a judgment that unbiasedly reflects nature or the sensible world. It is independent of what is personal or private in our apprehension and feelings. In other words, the judgment is free from personal feelings or prejudice; it is non-subjective.

From the above definition of principle, then, the main entry, the authorship, and the literary units principles should be fundamental truths in themselves. Also, the rules for the choice of entry based on such principles should be regulations or accepted procedures adopted for the application of the principles. The rules should, in particular, always result in the choice of an author as the main entry and in the choice of all the other author entries necessary for assembling literary units. The choice of the entries resulting from the rules must be free from personal feelings, prejudice and bias.

The investigation described below was designed to study the principle of main entry as well as the other principles dependent on it—the authorship and literary unit principles—in relation to the rules for the choice of entry in the *AACR*. The study was made in terms of the "objectivity" of the rules in determining the author main entries that will assemble literary units. The purpose of the investigation was to examine the validity of the above principles and to ask whether or not the cataloging rules should be based on them. Another purpose of the study was to discover any problems in the *AACR* that impair the determination of authorship or the assembly of literary units. A final purpose was to ask whether or not we need at all rules that make provisions for the choice of the main entry.

The investigation that was conducted was a systematic analysis of the first thirty-two rules of the *AACR* 1967, American edition. A systematic analysis is defined as a logical analysis of a given system, in this case the

70

system is represented by the *AACR* rules. Such an analysis includes an evaluation of the efficiency, accuracy, and productivity of the existing rules and procedures as measured against the established functions of the rules, and includes as well the design to new methods and procedures to improve the flow of decision-making through the rules. Actually, the systematic analysis used involved three different detailed and complex analyses. A full description of these analyses and their results is given in Chapters IV through VI.

The first analysis, presented in Chapter IV, is concerned with the validity of the authorship principle and the success or failure of the rules in determining main author entries. This analysis is a statistical one, enumerating rules resulting in main author entries.

Chapter V is devoted to studying the validity of the literary units principle as assembled by the rules. Again, this is a statistical analysis of the author entries chosen according to each rule—entries that can contribute to the assembling of literary units.

Finally, Chapter VI is devoted to the third analysis. In this chapter the objectivity of the rules is examined on the basis of their organization, structure and relationships to each other. This analysis makes use of flowcharting, a systems analysis technique.

The four analyses described above required careful examination of each rule, both individually and in relation to the other rules. As the investigation was begun, it became clear that each subrule, or exception to a rule, had to be considered as an entity in itself. That is, each part of a rule was concerned either with a special type of authorship, or it treated a certain kind of publication. For example, under Rule 3 for "shared authorship," subrule 3A deals with works of shared authorship whose principle author is indicated. Subrule 3B1 is for the same type of works but where the principle author is not indicated and the authors are not more than three. On the other hand, while both subrules 3B1a and 3B1b are concerned with the same type of authorship treated by subrule 3B1, these are for different types of publications. The first is for publications appearing in more than one volume, and the second is for those which appear in different editions. Considering their nature, the decision was made to study each of the subrules or exceptions to a rule as a rule by itself—with the result that 129 "rules" were to be studied instead of those numbered 1-32 in *AACR*.

Delimitation of the Study

The scope of the investigation has been suggested by the above description of method. Only the rules for choice of "entry" in the *AACR* 1967 were studied. The rules for form of heading or for description were included only if they affected the choice of entry. One further limitation should be pointed out. The British edition of the *AACR* 1967 was not included in the study. The investigation was concerned with the principle of the main entry as such, and the variations between the American and the British editions were not the concern of the study. In other words, the study was concerned with the main entry as a principle and with the question of

71

whether a set of rules in any code should be devoted to its choice. Another reason for limiting the study in this manner is the fact that the American edition is probably the most widely used and the most criticized.

FOOTNOTES

[1] Arthur Hugh Chaplin, *Tradition and Principle in Library Cataloguing* (Toronto: University of Toronto School of Library Science, 1968), p. 6.

[2] ICCP, *Report*, p. 19.

[3] Andrew D. Osborn, "AA Cataloging Code," pp. 3523-25.

[4] *AACR*, p. 258.

[5] *Ibid.*, p. 1.

[6] *Ibid.*

[7] "Revising the Rules," *Catalogue & Index*, No. 20 (October 1970), 3.

[8] Hines, *op. cit.*; Osborn, "AA Cataloging Code," p. 3525.

[9] "Revising the Rules," *Catalogue & Index*, No. 19 (July 1970), 3.

[10] "Danger—Code Erosion! An Anglo-American Exchange of Notes," *Catalogue & Index*, No. 14 (April 1969), 1.

[11] "Revising the Cataloguing Rules," *Catalogue & Index*, No. 15 (July 1969), 3.

[12] Hines, *op. cit.*, p. 62.

[13] Chaplin, *op. cit.*, p. 6.

[14] *AACR*, p. 3.

[15] C. D. Gull, "The Impact of Electronics upon Cataloging Rules," in ICCP, *Report*, pp. 281-90.

[16] Ralph H. Parker, "Book Catalogs," *Library Resources & Technical Services*, VIII (Fall 1964), 348.

[17] *The Code and the Cataloguer, Proceedings of the Colloquium on the Anglo-American Cataloguing Rules Held at the School of Library Science, University of Toronto on March 31 and April 1, 1967*, ed. by Katherine H. Packer, Delores Phillips, and Katharine L. Ball (Toronto: University of Toronto Press, 1969), p. 94.

[18] Osborn, "AA Cataloging Code," p. 3525.

[19] Hines, *op. cit.*, p. 63.

[20] Elizabeth Tate, review of *Anglo-American Cataloging Rules, Library Quarterly*, XXXVII (October 1967), 394.

[21] *Ibid.*

[22] Maurice B. Line, "White Elephants Revisited," *Catalogue & Index*, No. 13 (January 1969), 6.

[23] *Seminar on the Anglo-American Cataloguing Rules (1967), Proceedings of the Seminar Organized by the Cataloguing and Indexing Group of the Library Association at the University of Nottingham, 22nd—25th March,*

1968, ed. by J. C. Downing and N. F. Sharp (London: Library Association, 1969).

[24] *New Rules for an Old Game, Proceedings of a Workshop on the 1967 Anglo-American Cataloguing Code Held by the School of Librarianship, the University of British Columbia, April 13 and 14, 1967*, ed. by Thelma E. Allen and Daryl Ann Dickman (Vancouver: Publications Centre, University of British Columbia, 1967).

[25] *The Code and the Cataloguer.*

[26] C. Donald Cook, ed., "The New Rules in Action: A Symposium," *Library Resources & Technical Services*, XIII (Winter 1969), 7-41.

[27] P. R. Lewis and G. E. Hamilton, "Revising the Rules," *Catalogue & Index*, No. 20 (October 1970), 3.

[28] Chaplin, *op. cit.*, p. 7.

[29] S. R. Ranganathan, "The End of Superimposition?" *Catalogue & Index*, No. 18 (April 1970), 13.

[30] Nitecki, *op. cit.*, p. 256.

[31] *AACR*, p. 5.

[32] *Ibid.*, p. 9.

[33] Friedman and Jeffreys, *op. cit.*, p. 245.

[34] Ayres, *et. al.*, *op. cit.*, p. 267.

CHAPTER IV

DETERMINATION OF AUTHORSHIP

Methodology

The purpose of the analysis described in this chapter is to study statistically the validity of the authorship principle as reflected by the rules, and in particular to establish whether or not the rules provide guidance in determining the authorship of a publication and selecting a main entry under the author.

The criterion on which this analysis is developed is the following: in order to say that a rule is based on the authorship principle, the rule must result in the choice of an author (if such exists) as the main entry for the publication being cataloged.

Each of the 129 rules was carefully examined from the point of view of this criterion. It became obvious soon after the examination began that not all the rules result in the choice of an author as a main entry. This can happen even when the author's name appears on the title page of a publication. For example, while the author may be named on the title page of a publication, Rules 2A and 3B2 enter the publication under title, and Rule 20A enters it under a form heading. Further, there are other rules that allow a choice between an author and other types of entries. For example, Rules 4A and 5A specify the main entry under either the author (i.e., editor or compiler) or the title.

The above observations suggest that a distinction is made between two different groups of main entries. The first group is "author main entries," consisting of all entries under an author, personal or corporate. The second group is "substitute for the author" entries. It consists of main entries under something other than the real authors, whether personal or corporate, of a publication. These entries are of four different kinds:

1. *Substitute author.* This refers to a person or a corporate body that is not the real author of a publication. A substitute author is chosen as the main entry for some relationship he bears to the publication, other than intellectual responsibility. An example of this is legal publications, where a main entry is made under the defendant in a law suit.

2. *Title.* Main entries are made under the title-page title of the publication in hand.

3. *Form heading or uniform heading.* This is exemplified by a

publication that is entered according to its form or subject content. For example, the entry "U.S. Constitution" is a form heading entry. Also included in this group is *conventional name.* Here the entry is under "a name, other than the real or official name, by which a person, corporate body, place, or thing has come to be best known."[1] This occurs only once in Rule 25C2.

4. *Uniform title.* Main entry is made under "the particular title by which a work that has appeared under varying titles is to be identified for cataloging purposes."[2]

The first analysis of the rules with respect to the authorship principle is summarized in Table 2. The table shows for each rule the possible main entries it determines. The rules are listed in the chart according to their sequential order in the Code. There are two columns for main entries corresponding to the two major groups of entries, "author" and "substitute for the author" entries. In each of the columns the type of author entry prescribed by the corresponding rule is recorded either by an "x", or, in the case of types of author, by an abbreviated form of the type of author.

Analysis

The analysis shows that the rules can be grouped into three categories according to the degree to which they determine author main entries.

The first category consists of rules that are based on the authorship principle in that they *definitely* permit the choice of an author as a main entry.

The second comprises those rules which could possibly result in the choice of an author as the main entry.

The third consists of those rules which do not result in the choice of an author as a main entry.

The summary of the analysis of the rules into these three groups is shown in Table 3 below.

As can be seen, only a few of the rules, 28.6 percent, definitely determine author entries; 19.4 percent of the rules possibly determine author entries; and 52 percent, or the majority of the rules, do not determine author entries. In other words, the rules are not generally based on the determination of authorship responsibility, as it is claimed in the introduction to the rules.[3]

A more detailed analysis of the above three groups of rules is given in Tables 4, 5, and 6 below, to show what types of entries are provided by the rules in each group and to clarify why certain rules do not result in an author main entry. Table 4 shows those rules which definitely allow the choice of an author as a main entry. The certainty about authorship determination results from the fact that the rules are structured so that either a single author is determined or, in the case of multiple or shared authorship, a choice is made between one author and another. Of the thirty-seven rules in this group, thirty either select a single author or allow for a choice between authors on the basis of principal responsibility or order of arrangement on the title page. Of the remaining seven rules, for three the choice is between a personal author and a corporate body; for another three it is between the author and a

TABLE 2
MAIN ENTRY AS DETERMINED BY RULES

Rule Number	Author	Substitutes for the Author			
		Substitute Author	Title	Form Heading	Uniform Title
1A	Author				
1B	Author				
2A			x		
2B	Author				
2C			x		
3A	Author				
3B1	Author				
3B1a	Author				
3B1b	Author				
3B1c			x		
3B2			x		
3C1	—	—	—	—	—
3C2			x		
4A	Editor		x		
5A	Editor		x		
5B	Editor		x		
6A			x		
6B1			x		
6B1 Ex	Corporate Body				
6B2	Corporate Body				
6C	Corporate Body				
6D1	—	—	—	—	—
6D2	—	—	—	—	—
7A		x			
7B					x
7C		Adapter			
8A	Artist/Author of Text				
8B	Author				
8C	Artist				
8D1	Author of Text				
8D2	Artist	E	x		
8E1	Artist				
8E2		Person Responsible for Cat.			
9A	Author of Biography/ Author of Work				

TABLE 2 (cont'd.)

Rule Number	Author	Substitutes for the Author			
		Substitute Author	Title	Form Heading	Uniform Title
9B	Author of Work				
10	Calligrapher				
11A	Commentator		x		
11B	Author		x		
11C	Author/ Commentator		x		
12		Praeses Proponent Defendant Respondent			
13A		Reporter			
13B		Participant	x		
13C		Reporter			
14A	Original Author				
14B	Reviser				
15A	Author/Trans- lator				
15B	Editor (Trans- lator)				
16A		Nominal Author			
16B	Writer (i.e., Author)				
17A1	Personal Author/ Corporate Body				
17A2	Corporate Body				
17B	Personal Author		x		
17C1a				x	
17C1b	Corporate Body		x		
17C1c				x	
17C2a	Personal Author				
17C2b	Editor		x		
17C2c	Personal Author	Editor	x		
18A	Corporate Body (Parent Body)/ Corporate Body (Subordinate Unit)				
18B	Corporate Body (Parent Body)				

TABLE 2 (cont'd.)

Rule Number	Author	Substitutes for the Author			
		Substitute Author	Title	Form Heading	Uniform Title
18C	Corporate Body (Subordinate Unit)				
18D	Corporate Body (Parent Body)		x		
19A			x		
19B			x		
19B Ex1		Composer	x		
19B Ex2	Personal Author				
19B Ex3	Composer				
20A				x	
20B1				x	
20B2	Compiler		x		
20C	Personal Author/ Corporate Body				
20D	Editor		x		x
21A	Corporate Body				
21B	Corporate Body			x	
22A1				x	
22A2				x	
22B	Personal Author/ Corporate Body		x		
22B Ex				x	
22C	Personal Author/ Corporate Body				
22D				x	
23A				x	
23B				x	
23C				x	
23D				x	
23E	Personal Author/ Corporate Body		x		
24A				x	
24B		Commentator		x	
25A1				x	
25A2a				x	
25A2b				x	
25B1				x	
25B2	Corporate Body				
25C1				x	
25C2				x	

TABLE 2 (cont'd.)

Rule Number	Author	Substitutes for the Author			
		Substitute Author	Title	Form Heading	Uniform Title
25D			x		
25E1				x	
25E2				x	
25F1				x	
25F2				x	
25F3				x	
25F4	Editor		x		
26A1	Corporate Body				
26A2	Corporate Body		x		
26B	Author		x		
26C1a (1)		Person Bringing Action			
26C1a (2)		Person Bringing Appeal			
26C1b		Person Prosecuted			
26C1c	Defendant				
26C1d		Court			
26C1e		Court			
26C1f		Judge			
26C2a		Party			
26C2b		Attorney			
27A					x
27B					x
28					x
29A1				x	
29A2				x	
29A3	Personal Author/ Corporate Body		x	x	
29B				x	
29C				x	
30A			x		
30B				x	
30C	Editor		T		
31A	Personal Author			x	
31A Ex	Author				
31B				x	
32A				x	
32B	Compiler				x

TABLE 3

DEGREE TO WHICH RULES 1-32 AND THEIR SUBRULES
DETERMINE AUTHOR MAIN ENTRIES

Author Main Entry Determination	Number of Rules	Percentages
Definite	37	28.6
Possible	25	19.4
Not Possible	67	52.0
TOTAL	129	100.0

TABLE 4

TYPE OF AUTHORSHIP
AS DEFINITELY DETERMINED BY THE RULES

ME Under:	Rules 1-6 and their Subrules	Rules 7-19 and their Subrules	Rules 20-26 and their Subrules	Rules 27-32 and their Subrules	Total
A	11	15	3	1	30
PA or CB		1	2		3
A or Coll		3			3
PB or SU		1			1
TOTAL	11	20	5	1	37

Abbreviations used:

ME	Main Entry	PA	Personal Author
A	Author	PB	Parent Body
CB	Corporate Body	SU	Subordinate Unit
Coll	Collaborator		

collaborator; and for one a choice is made between a parent body and a subordinate unit.

Table 5 gives a statistical summary of the rules which possibly (that is, in some cases), can result in the choice of an author as the main entry for a publication. The uncertainty here is due to the fact that the determination of

TABLE 5

**TYPE OF AUTHOR MAIN ENTRIES
AS POSSIBLY DETERMINED BY THE RULES**

ME Under:	Rules 1-6 and their Subrules	Rules 7-19 and their Subrules	Rules 20-26 and their Subrules	Rules 27-32 and their Subrules	Total
A or T	3	8	4	1	16
A or T or Ed		2			2
A or T or S		1			1
A or FH			1	1	2
A or T or UH			1		1
PA or CB or T			2		2
PA or CB or FH				1	1
TOTAL	3	11	8	3	25

Abbreviations used:

ME	Main Entry	S	Substitute for the Author
A	Author	PA	Personal Author
Ed	Editor	UH	Uniform Heading
CB	Corporate Body	T	Title
FH	Form Heading		

the main entry by all rules of this group is based upon a choice between one or two authors and some other entity which is not an author, such as title, form heading, uniform title, or substitute for the author. As the table shows, of the twenty-five rules in this group, sixteen, or the majority, allow for a choice between the author and the title of a book. For two rules the choice is between the author and a form heading. And for each of the remaining seven rules, one of three different entities is chosen. For example, two rules allow for a choice between the author, the title and the editor; two other rules force a decision between a personal author, a corporate body, and the title.

Table 6 summarizes the rules which do not allow for an author main entry. The rules in this group are of three different types. Those of the first type, representing the majority, or fifty-eight rules, categorically determine a non-author main entry. Twenty-eight of these rules enter the work being cataloged under form heading, fourteen under substitute author, eight under title, five under uniform title, two under uniform heading and one under conventional name. The second type of rule allows for a choice between one

TABLE 6

TYPES OF MAIN ENTRY OTHER THAN AUTHOR
AS DETERMINED BY THE RULES

ME Under:	Rules 1-6 and their Subrules	Rules 7-19 and their Subrules	Rules 20-26 and their Subrules	Rules 27-32 and their Subrules	Total
T	6		1	1	8
FH		2	19	7	28
UT		1		4	5
UH			2		2
CN			1		1
SA		5	9		14
SA or T		4			4
SA or SC		1			1
SA or FH			1		1
No Entry	3				3
TOTAL	9	13	33	12	67

Abbreviations used:

ME	Main Entry	SC	Substitute Collaborator
CN	Conventional Name	T	Title
FH	Form Heading	UH	Uniform Heading
SA	Substitute Author	UT	Uniform Title

non-author entry and another. There are six such rules. For four of these the choice is between a substitute author and the title; for one, between one substitute author and another; and for one, between a substitute author and a form heading. The third type is represented by only three rules. Rules of this type do not provide any main entry at all inasmuch as they are designed for establishing the form of heading.

A further analysis of authorship determination can be made by groups of rules, e.g., General Rules, Works with Authorship of Mixed Character, Certain Legal Publications, and Certain Religious Publications. A summary of this analysis is given in Table 7. The table shows that the degree to which the authorship principle is applied and the success or failure of the rules in providing author main entries vary greatly from one group of rules to another.

TABLE 7

DETERMINATION OF AUTHOR MAIN ENTRIES
BY GROUPS OF RULES

Author Main entry Determination	Rules 1-6 and their Subrules		Rules 7-19 and their Subrules		Rules 20-26 and their Subrules		Rules 27-32 and their Subrules	
	No.	%	No.	%	No.	%	No.	%
Definite	11	47.8	20	45.4	5	11.0	1	6.3
Possible	3	13.0	11	25.0	8	17.3	3	18.7
Not Possible	9	39.2	13	29.6	33	71.7	12	75.0
TOTAL	23	100.0	44	100.0	46	100.0	16	100.0

General Rules 1-6 and their Subrules
This group, which includes twenty-five rules, ranks first with regard to the number of rules which definitely allow an author to be selected for main entry. Eleven, or 47.8 percent, of these rules result in an author main entry, either through determination of a single author or through a choice between one author and another (see Table 4). As to possible author main entries, the General Rule group ranks fourth, with 13 percent of its rules structured around the choice between an author and a non-author main entry (see Table 5). Finally, it ranks third with respect to the number of rules (39.2 percent) that do not allow an author main entry to be selected. Six of these rules provide main entry under title while three rules are for establishing form of heading (see Table 6).

Works with Authorship of Mixed Character,
Rules 7-19 and their Subrules
This group of forty-four rules is possibly the most successful one in contributing author main entries in that it has the fewest rules (29.6 percent) resulting in non-author main entries. Most of the rules in this group are structured around the choice between one type of entry and another. With 45.4 percent of its rules providing author main entries, this group ranks second in definitely determining author main entries. Generally the choice allowed in these rules is between one author and another (see Table 4). With regard to possible determination of author main entries, the group ranks first, with 25 percent of its rules prescribing a choice between an author and a non-author main entry (see Table 5).

Certain Legal Publications,
Rules 20-26 and their Subrules
In this group of forty-six rules the possibility of having an author as a

83

main entry decreases considerably. Only 28.3 percent of the rules could result in an author main entry. Of these, 11 percent definitely prescribe author main entries, while 17.3 percent, depending on the work being cataloged, make such entries allowable. This group ranks third with respect to definite determination and third with respect to possible determination of main author entries. It is the second largest group of rules non-determinative of author main entries, with 71.7 percent of its rules providing main entries other than author entries (see Table 6).

Certain Religious Publications,
Rules 27-32 and their Subrules

As can be seen from Table 7, this new group of sixteen rules contributes least to the determination of author main entries. Only 25 percent of its rules could result in an author main entry. This percentage breaks down into 6.3 percent of the rules providing for definite and 18.7 percent for possible author main entries. This group therefore ranks fourth with regard to the former category and second with regard to the latter. It ranks first in the number of rules (75 percent) providing non-author main entries (see Table 6).

In summary, it is evident from the above analysis that the authorship principle is not a general principle and does not result in the uniform entry; consequently, it is not a sound principle on which to structure a set of cataloging rules. As was seen, many of the rules for choice of entry in the *AACR* are not designed to provide a main entry under the author, in some cases even when the author's name appears on the title page of the publication. It is misleading to say that these rules are based on the authorship principle.

It was also seen that the degree of consistency in adherence to the authorship principle varies greatly from one group of rules to another. The rules for "authorship of mixed character" seem to be better designed to meet the authorship criterion than rules in any of the other groups. The "general rules" are second in meeting this criterion, with a substantial number of rules determining author main entries. On the other hand, the rules for "certain legal publications" and "certain religious publications" are, in general, much less consistent in providing main entry under author. These two groups are based on special types of materials and therefore rules for cataloging them incorporate many exceptions to the general rules and principles.

FOOTNOTES

[1] *AACR*, p. 347.
[2] *Ibid.*, p. 344.
[3] *Ibid.*, p. 5.

CHAPTER V

LITERARY UNITS

Methodology

Lubetzky claimed that the *AACR* is "characterized by a body of principles rooted in the objectives which the catalogue of a library is assumed to serve...."[1] The second objective of the catalog, according to Lubetzky, deals with literary units. He explains this objective by saying that the aim of the catalog is "to reveal to the user of the catalogue what editions (and translations) the library has of a given work and what works of a given author." This is the definition of literary unit which is used in the present study. Lubetzky's claim that the main entry is necessary for assembling literary units and, therefore, is defensible in the Code has been invalidated by the results of the previous chapter. We have seen, for instance, that not all the rules result in main entries under author. That is, in all cases where the rules fail to provide an author entry, there can be no assembly of literary units.

The purpose of this chapter is to focus more particularly on the literary unit principle as a sound and valid reason for the existence of the main entry and the rules for the choice of entry in the *AACR*. Before discussing the methodology for analyzing the elements of the rules, it should be noted that form of heading (whether it is a main or an added entry) and cross references play the major roles in assembling literary units. Authors (personal or corporate) quite often change their names, or write under different names. Literary units in this case can be obtained either by entering all the works of an author under one form of his name and making the necessary cross references, (i.e., *see* references) from all the other forms of the name; or by entering each individual work under either of the forms of the author's name with *see also* references made from one form to the other. An example of the use of *see also* references to assemble literary units is the following: Rule 42B is for selection between an author's real name and one of his several pseudonyms. Footnote 5 to this rule, which is an alternative rule, states:

> If the works of an author appear under several pseudonyms or under his real name and one or more pseudonyms, enter each work under the name he used for it. Make *see also* references to connect the names.[2]

It is obvious here that the main entry does not assemble literary units; rather the *see also* reference performs this function by linking the various forms of an author's name. Similar provisions are made in Rules 6D and 68 for corporate bodies with several forms of names.

It is assumed in this study that the selection of the form of heading and the making of cross references are done in such a way as to insure the integrity of literary units. Form of heading and cross references are properly the subject of Chapters 2, 3, and 5 of *AACR* and are not considered in this study, which investigates only the selection of main and added author entries that contribute to assembling literary units.

As indicated, literary units do not result from main entries alone. They are attained through a combination of various elements. These are 1) main entries, 2) added entries, and 3) cross references. It is necessary, therefore, to study the rules with respect to all three of those elements. The present analysis was designed to answer the following questions: Are the rules structured to result in literary units? Are they successful in attaining this objective? To what degree? What are the elements assigned by the rules which assemble these units? And finally, how complete are the literary units resulting from the rules?

The criterion on which the analysis was designed is as follows: a rule will be considered successful and well structured if it results in all necessary main and added author entries required to preserve the integrity of literary units. According to this criterion, any of the rules described earlier which provide substitutes for the author entries, with the exception of the substitute author, do not satisfy this criterion in that they do not provide for author entries.

To determine the success or failure of each rule in assembling literary units, each rule was examined to study statistically the elements assigned by the rules. The following case studies illustrate this method.

Case Study No. 1

Rule 3A states:
Enter a work of shared authorship under the person or corporate body, if any, to whom principal authorship is attributed, e.g., by wording or typography. Make added entries under the other authors involved if there are not more than two. Always make an added entry under an author, other than the principal author, whose name appears first on the title page.[3]

This rule yields two kinds of entries that assemble literary units. There are a main entry under the principal author and added entry (or entries) under other authors if they are not more than two. It is also important to note that the literary units resulting from this rule could be incomplete. For example, when the other authors are more than two, only one added entry will be provided and that under the first-named author (after the principal author). Therefore, no literary units will be assembled for all authors named on the title page other than the principal author and the first-named author.

Case Study No. 2

Rule 3B2 states:
If no one is presented as a principal author and there are more than three authors, enter the work under its title unless the work is produced under the direction of an editor named on the title page. In this case apply Rule 4. Make an added entry under the author named first on the title page.[4]

In this rule only one element, an added entry under the first-named author on the title page, contributes to the assembling of literary units. Like the first case study, this rule does not give complete literary units, since no added entries are made for any author other than the first.

Case Study No. 3

Rule 23A states:
Enter court rules under the name of the jurisdiction from which the court derives its authority followed by the subheading *Court rules* and the name of the court governed by the rules. Make a see also reference from the heading of the court. . . . Make an added entry under the promulgating body if it is other than the court governed by the rules.[5]

Two elements are provided in this rule for assembling literary units. The first is a *see also* reference from the heading of the court. The second is an added entry under the promulgating body if it is other than the court governed by it. The main entry in this rule does not contribute to the formation of literary units since it is a form heading.

Case Study No. 4

Rule 1A states:
Enter a work, a collection of works, or selections from works by one author under the person or corporate body that is the author, whether named in the work or not . . .[6]

Only one element, a main entry under the author, is provided to assemble literary units. The literary unit here is definitely complete since there is only one author—that is, there is no question of authors not represented by added entries.

As the examination of each rule was finished it was found that the rules could be grouped into seven categories according to the kinds of elements assigned to give literary units. These seven categories are:
1. Rules that provide only the main entry element;
2. Rules that provide only the added entry element;
3. Rules that provide both main and added entry elements;
4. Rules that provide the main entry and cross reference elements;
5. Rules that provide the added entry and cross reference elements;

6. Rules that provide the main entry, added entry and cross reference elements; and

7. Rules that do not provide for any of the elements listed above.

In the examination of rules it was also found that the literary units resulting from many of the rules which provide one or more of the elements were incomplete. This was particularly true when a rule does not provide added entries under all the authors or collaborators listed on the title page of a given publication.

In some cases there were problems in determining whether or not some of the elements provided by the rules could actually be considered elements contributing to literary units. Rules 26C1a(1) through 26C2b, for instance, direct that publications be entered under certain persons or corporate bodies who are connected with the publication in some way other than being responsible for intellectual content. The entry under the defendant in court is an illustration of this. Although the defendant is responsible for the existence of the case, he is not responsible for the intellectual content of the proceedings of the case. This type of author entry, while considered a substitute author entry, is more properly a subject entry.

Another problem in determining whether a rule provided literary unit elements results from the fact that, although some rules do not specify added entries in the body of their text, these added entry elements can be extracted from the examples illustrating the rules. Cases where this occurs can be seen in Rules 23B, 27A, and 24A2.

Table 8 records the data resulting from the examination of the rules. In this table the first column lists each rule according to its sequential order in the Code. The second column, headed "Elements of Literary Units," is subdivided into the three different elements required for complete literary units: main author entry (MAE), added author entry (AAE), and cross references (XR). The completeness of the units provided by each rule is recorded in the third column under the general question "Literary unit complete?" Data about the presence of certain elements and the completeness of literary units are recorded under "yes" or "no" headings. This format is useful because it allows space to code additional information about why certain elements do not exist, why a certain element does not contribute to building a literary unit, and why a certain literary unit is incomplete (see Table 8 footnote).

Analysis

The analysis relating to the objective of assembling literary units reveals that the rules are not completely successful in attaining this objective. In many cases they fail to provide the necessary main and/or added author entry elements required for complete literary units.

The analysis also shows that the principle which makes the literary unit a function of the main entry is an unsound and invalid principle. The role of the main entry in this regard is minor. More important are the added entries that account for the majority of the elements required for the assembly of literary units.

TABLE 8
COMPLETENESS OF LITERARY UNITS
PER EXISTING RULES*

Rule Number	Elements of Literary Units						Literary Unit Complete?	
	MAE		AAE		XR			
	Yes	No	Yes	No	Yes	No	Yes	No
1A	x						x	
1B	x		x				x	
2A		T	x					1
2B	x		x		x		x	
2C		FoH	x		x		x	
3A	x		x					1
3B1	x		x				x	
3B1a	x		x				x	
3B1b	x		x				x	
3B1c		T	x					2
3B2		T	x					1
3C1	x		x		x		x	
3C2		T	x		x			2
4A	x		x					3
5A	x		x					1
5B	x		x					1
6A		T						
6B1		T	x				x	
6B1 Exc	x						x	
6B2	x						x	
6C	x						x	
6D1		FoH						
6D2		T	x				x	
7A	x		x					4
7B		UT	x			UT		
7C	x		x				x	
8A	x		x				x	
8B	x		x					5
8C	x		x				x	
8D1	x		x					6
8D2	x		x					1
8E1	x		x					1
8E2	x		x				x	
9A	x		x				x	
9B	x		x				x	
10	x		x				x	
11A	x		x					1
11B	x		x					1

TABLE 8 (cont'd.)

Rule Number	Elements of Literary Units						Literary Unit Complete?	
	MAE		AAE		XR			
	Yes	No	Yes	No	Yes	No	Yes	No
11C	x		x					1
12	x		x				x	
13A	x		x					1
13B	x		x					1
13C	x		x				x	
14A	x		x				x	
14B	x		x		x		x	
15A	x		x					7
15B	x		x					1
16A	x		x				x	
16B	x							8
17A1	x		x					1
17A2	x		x				x	
17B	x		x					2
17C1a		FH						
17C1b	x			FH				2
17C2a	x						x	
17C2b	x		x					1
17C2c	x		x					1
18A	x				x		x	
18B	x						x	
18C	x		x				x	
18D	x		x					1
19A	x		x					2
19B	x		x					2
19B Exc 1	x		x				x	
19B Exc 2	x						x	
19B Exc 3	x						x	
20A		FH	x		x		x	
20B1		FH	x		x		x	
20B2	x			FH			x	
20C	x						x	
20D	x		x		x			1
21A	x			FH			x	
21B	x		x				x	
22A1		FH		FH				
22A2		FH		FH				
22B	x		x				x	
22B Exc		FH		FH				

90

TABLE 8 (cont'd.)

Rule Number	Elements of Literary Units						Literary Unit Complete?	
	MAE		AAE		XR			
	Yes	No	Yes	No	Yes	No	Yes	No
22C	X						X	
22D		FH						
23A		FH	X		X		X	
23B		FH	X					9
23C		FH		FH				
23D		FH	X					2,10
23E	X		X					2,10
24A		FH	X				X	
24B	X		X				X	
25A1		FH	X				X	
25A2a		FH		FH				
25A2b		UT		FH				
25B1		FH		FH				
25B2	X		X				X	
25C1		FH		FH				
25C2		FH		FH				
25D		T	X					1
25E1		FH		FH				
25E2		FH		FH				
25F1		FH	X					10
25F2		FH	X					10
25F3		FH	X					10
25F4	X		X					1
26A1	X		X				X	
26A2	X		X					1
26B	X		X				X	
26C1a(1)	X		X					1
26C1a(2)	X		X					2
26C1b	X		X					1
26C1c	X		X					1
26C1d	X		X					3
26C1e	X		X					3
26C1f	X		X					3
26C2a	X		X				X	
26C2b	X		X					11
27A		UT	X		X			4
27B		FH	X				X	
28		UT		UT				
29A1		FH	X				X	

TABLE 8 (cont'd.)

| Rule Number | Elements of Literary Units | | | | | | Literary Unit Complete? | |
| | MAE | | AAE | | XR | | | |
	Yes	No	Yes	No	Yes	No	Yes	No
29A2		FH	x					9
29A3	x		x					1
29B		FH		FH				
29C		FH		FH				
30A		FH						
30B		FH	x					10
30C	x		x					1
31A	x							12
31A Exc	x						x	
31B		FH	x					10,1
32A		FH						
32B	x			FH			x	

*When a rule does not provide a literary unit element, such as a MAE or AAE, then those elements (not literary unit elements) which were provided by the rule are recorded in the appropriate "no" column in abbreviated form.

Abbreviations used:

MAE	Main Author Entry	FH	Form Heading
AAE	Added Author Entry	FoH	Form of Heading
XR	Cross Reference	UT	Uniform Title
T	Title		

There were twelve different ways a literary unit could be incomplete. These are numbered. When a literary unit was incomplete the number signifying the reason for incompleteness was recorded in the "no" column. These twelve types of incompleteness are the following:

1. Added entries are made for only the first-named author if there are more than three.
2. Rules refer to other rules which in turn either result in incomplete literary units or make unclear provisions.
3. Added entries are made for only the first-named author regardless of the number of authors on the title page.
4. Complete with exception.
5. An added entry is made for the illustrator only if the illustrations are a noteworthy feature of the work (Rule 8B).
6. No added entry is made for an artist in the case of a reproduction of his work accompanied by a commentary (Rule 8D1).
7. Added entries are not always provided for a translator (Rule 15A).
8. No added entry is made for the person who presents a speech written by another person (Rule 16B).
9. Added entries are not required by the rule; however, the example illustrating the rule provides an added entry (Rule 23B, 29A2).
10. An added entry is made for an editor or compiler only if named on the title page.
11. Added entries are not made for all the parties involved (Rule 26C2b).
12. Some of the official acts of popes, bishops, etc. do not appear under their names, but rather under their offices (Rule 31A).

Cross references were suggested by some of the rules. It appears from the analysis that cross references play a minor role in assembling literary units. This is not true, however, since they are suggested only when for some reason it is deemed necessary that they should be included in the rules for the choice of entry to assist in assembling the literary units. Cross references definitely play a major role in assembling literary units, and they are treated more comprehensively in Chapter 5 of *AACR*, which is beyond the scope of this study.

Table 9 shows a statistical summary of elements in the rules that contribute to assembling literary units. It shows that the rules provide literary unit elements in 82.95 percent of the cases. In other words, out of the 129 rules studied, twenty-two do not provide any of the elements that assemble literary units. Table 8 shows that the elements provided by these twenty-two rules are either titles, uniform titles, or form headings, none of which are author entries.

TABLE 9

STATISTICAL SUMMARY OF ELEMENTS
IN RULES DETERMINATIVE OF LITERARY UNITS

Elements Determinative of Literary Units	Number of Rules and Subrules	Percentages
MAE	16	12.40
MAE + AAE	62	48.06
MAE + XR	2	1.50
MAE + AAE + XR	3	2.30
AAE	18	13.30
AAE + XR	6	4.60
None	22	17.05
TOTALS	129	100.00

As mentioned, the role of the main entry taken by itself is minimal in determining literary unit elements. Table 9 makes it clear that a few rules (sixteen, or 12.4 percent) establish literary unit elements by main entry (MAE) alone. In the majority of the cases (70.55 percent) literary units are obtained through a combination of main entries, added entries (AAE), and cross references (XR). The rules that determine literary units by the use of main and added entries (MAE and AAE) are 48.06 percent of the total. Second in frequency are rules providing literary unit elements by added entries (AAE) alone; 13.3 percent of the rules are in this category. Then come the 12.4 percent of the rules in which the main entry alone determines literary units. Four point six percent of the rules achieve this objective by both added entries and cross references, 2.3 percent by main entry in combination with added entries and cross references, and 1.5 percent by main entries and cross references.

Looking at the rules resulting in literary units using main entries both alone and in combination with other entries, it can be seen that these number eighty-three, or 64.26 percent of the total. On the other hand, there are slightly more rules resulting in literary units using added entries either alone or in combination: eighty-nine, or 68.26 percent.

It is evident then that the main entry is only one of several elements used to effect the assembling of literary units. The majority of rules are structured around multiple choices between several elements or entries, as was brought out in the earlier discussion on the authorship principle.

An analysis similar to that just done for the total group of rules can be performed on special subgroups of rules, e.g., "General Rules," "Works with Authorship of Mixed Character," "Certain Legal Publications," and "Certain Religious Publications." Table 10 shows that the elements determinative of literary units vary considerably from one group to another, with a resulting variation in the degree of success or failure of each of the groups in assembling literary units. A discussion of each of these groups of rules follows.

TABLE 10

STATISTICAL SUMMARY OF ELEMENTS
BY SUBGROUPS OF RULES DETERMINATIVE OF LITERARY UNITS

Elements Determinative of Literary Units	Rules 1-6 & Subrules		Rules 7-19 & Subrules		Rules 20-26 & Subrules		Rules 27-32 & Subrules	
	No.	%	No.	%	No.	%	No.	%
MAE	4	17.4	6	13.6	3	6.5	3	18.6
MAE + AAE	8	34.8	33	75.0	19	41.3	2	12.4
MAE + XR	1	4.3	1	2.3	0	0	0	0
MAE + AAE + XR	1	4.3	1	2.3	1	2.2	0	0
AAE	5	21.7	0	0	8	17.3	5	31.2
AAE + XR	2	8.7	0	0	3	6.5	1	6.2
None	2	8.7	3	6.8	12	26.0	5	31.2
TOTALS	23	100.0	44	100.0	46	100.0	16	100.0

General Rules, 1-6 and their Subrules

There are twenty-three rules in this group. Classifying these rules according to how they are determinative of literary units, it is seen that the highest percentage of rules provides for literary units by MAE + AAE at 34.8 percent, followed by rules using AAE alone at 21.7 percent, MAE alone at 17.4 percent, AAE + XR at 8.7 percent, and finally MAE + XR and MAE + AAE + XR, each at 4.3 percent. Rules that failed to provide any literary unit elements at all were in a minority, amounting to only 8.7 percent.

Works of Authorship of Mixed Character, Rules 7-19 and their Subrules

There are forty-four rules in this group. Rules providing MAE + AAE elements account for 75 percent of this subgroup. Those providing only the MAE element account for 13.6 percent, followed by those providing MAE + XR and MAE + AAE + XR, each at only 2.3 percent.

This substantial increase in the number of rules which provide MAE + AAE elements is due to the fact that most of the rules in this subgroup are structured around the choice of main entry between one author or another. An added entry is always made for the author not chosen as the main entry. Thus, literary units are assembled in this group of rules through the main entry element for one type of author and through the added entry element for another type. Rule 8A, for example, forces a choice for main entry between the artist and the author of a text. Then it requires that an added entry be made for the person not chosen for the main entry.

Rules that failed in providing any literary unit elements at all are very small in number. They represent only 6.8 percent of the rules in this group. Again, this is accounted for by the fact that the rules determine choice between authors in the case of mixed authorship, and rarely (only three rules) do they fail to specify a literary unit element. The three exceptions are Rules 7B, 17C1a and 17C1c; the first specifies MAE under Uniform Title, the other two specify Form Headings.

Certain Legal Publications Rules 20-26 and their Subrules

The number of rules in this subgroup is forty-six. As was the case for the first two groups, the largest number of rules in this group (41.3 percent) select MAE + AAE elements for assembling literary units. The next largest number of rules are those providing AAE elements (17.3 percent). Both MAE and AAE + XR elements are provided by 6.5 percent of the rules, and finally, 2.2 percent of the rules specify MAE + AAE + XR elements.

The number of rules specifying MAE + AAE elemets is so large because many of the rules in this group are structured to determine a choice between authors as main entries and also because the rules permit extensive use of form headings and uniform titles as main entries. The rules in this group which do not provide any elements required for literary units are large in number, accounting for 26 percent of the total. This again is due to the extensive use in this group of rules of form headings and uniform titles as main entries.

95

Certain Religious Publications
Rules 27-32 and their Subrules

There are sixteen rules in this subgroup. Unlike the previous three groups, the largest number of rules in this group specify AAE alone. These account for 31.2 percent of the rules, followed by the rules which specify MAE alone (18.6 percent), then MAE + AAE (12.4 percent), and lastly AAE + XR (6.2 percent).

Again, many rules in this group result in the use of form headings and uniform titles, which means that rules specifying added entries are the major source of literary unit elements in this group. It also accounts for the sizable number of rules (31.2 percent) which do not produce any of the author elements required for assembling literary units.

As can be seen from the above analysis, with the exception of the subgroup works with authorship of mixed character, the exceptions to the general rules are much less successful than the general rules themselves in assembling literary units.

Complete Versus Incomplete Literary Units

It was mentioned in Chapter III that in some instances incomplete literary units result from the application of a rule. This happens especially when a rule does not provide entries for all of the authors listed on the title page of a publication. The present analysis shows that not all of the rules produce complete literary units. As shown in Table 11 below, out of the 107 rules which contribute at least some element to the assembling of literary units, only fifty-three rules (49.5 percent) result in complete units. That is, fifty-four rules result in incomplete literary units.

TABLE 11

RULES RESULTING IN
COMPLETE AND INCOMPLETE LITERARY UNITS

Literary Units	Number of Rules	Percentages
Complete	53	49.5
Incomplete	54	50.5
TOTAL	107	100.0

The incompleteness varied in nature. As shown in the footnote to Table 8, there are twelve reasons why a literary unit can be incomplete. Four of these reasons are responsible for forty-four of the rules providing incomplete units. The remaining eight reasons cover only eight rules. A description of the major reasons why incompleteness of literary units occurs is given below.

1. The major reason for incompleteness of literary units results from those rules which require an added entry only for the first-named author when there are more than three authors on the title page. Twenty-seven rules are of this type.
2. Next in contributing to incompleteness are those rules which, in making provision for added entries, refer to other rules which in turn result in incomplete units, or whose stipulations for added entries are unclear. There are nine rules in this category.
3. Seven rules suggest added entries under editors or compilers only if these are named on the title page. This is contrary to the provisions for main entries stated in other rules—e.g., Rules 1 and 2, which suggest searching reference sources or checking other editions for establishing the entries.
4. Four rules determine the fourth major reason for incompleteness of literary units. These rules suggest added entries for only the first-named author regardless of the number of authors on the title page. In other words, the "rule of three" is not followed in this case.

Although the remaining eight reasons why rules result in incomplete literary units involve fewer rules and are thus not as important as those mentioned above, they might be reviewed briefly. All represent instances in which added entries are not made.

5. Two rules make exceptions for some types of publications—for instance, the Bible—by suggesting that added entries should not be made for individuals mentioned on the title page.
6. An added entry is made for an illustrator only if the illustrations are a noteworthy feature of the work (Rule 8B).
7. No added entry is made for an artist in the case of a reproduction of his work accompanied by a commentary (Rule 8D1).
8. Added entries are not always provided for a translator (Rule 15A).
9. No added entry is made for a person presenting a speech that is written by another person (Rule 16B).
10. Rules 23B and 29A2 do not require an added entry for an author; however, the examples suggest making added entries.
11. Added entries are not provided for all the parties involved—for instance, all the parties involved in a court case (Rule 26C2b).
12. Some of the official acts of popes, bishops, etc. do not appear under the names of these persons but rather under their offices (Rule 31A).

It might be noted that Rule 33 was not treated in the above analysis. This was because the use of Rule 33 for added entries does not contribute to the completeness of literary units, inasmuch as the rule offers the same guidelines specified in Rules 1-32. It is in fact nothing more than a grouping of these practices in one place.

Literary Units Under Subject Headings

A further observation suggested by the above analysis is that it is not possible to assemble complete literary units under subject headings. As mentined earlier, Lubetzky stressed the importance of the main entry as a means for assembling literary units under subject headings. Under subject headings these units can be obtained only through main entries. Thus, for the 34.95 percent of the rules (see Table 6) which do not specify author main entries, there is no possibility of attaining literary units under the subject headings. The main entries specified in these rules are titles, uniform titles, form headings, etc.

Even in the remaining 65.05 percent of the rules where an author main entry is specified, literary units under subject headings can still be incomplete. There are several reasons for this incompleteness.

1. Where multiple authorship is involved, no added entries under the subject heading are made for the authors or collaborators of the publication cataloged.

2. There are authors who write on various subjects, with the result that their books are scattered under different subject headings. Thus, all books by one author will never be assembled under one subject heading.

3. A work of fiction is not given a subject heading when cataloged, so the works of a fiction writer will never be assembled under any subject heading.

For reasons such as these the assembly of literary units under subject headings, as advocated by Lubetzky, seems to be a difficult objective to fulfill—one that cannot be accomplished with any reasonable degree of consistency.

FOOTNOTES

[1] Seymour Lubetzky, "Background and Underlying Principles," in *New Rules for an Old Game*, p. 29.

[2] *AACR*, pp. 74-75.

[3] *Ibid.*, p. 14.

[4] *Ibid.*, p. 16.

[5] *Ibid.*, p. 50.

[6] *Ibid.*, p. 11.

CHAPTER VI

THE EFFECT OF THE MAIN ENTRY PRINCIPLE
ON THE RULES FOR THE CHOICE OF ENTRY

Methodology

The two previous chapters have studied the authorship and literary unit principles in their relationship to the main entry. It is clear from the discussions in these chapters that neither principle is consistently adhered to and that the validity of both is questionable. Since the main entry is integral to the design of the *AACR*, it seems important now to study the objectivity and organization of the *AACR* rules in determining main entries. This chapter is therefore devoted to studying the decision-making processes involved in selecting the main entry according to Rules 1-32.

The analysis in this chapter is designed to answer the following questions: Is choosing an entry, according to the rules, a simple process? Or does it require a great amount of decision making? Are the rules organized in such a way as to make the decision-making process smooth? If a rule leaves unanswered questions with respect to choice of entry, does it lead to another rule that makes such a choice possible? Are the rules discrete or do they overlap? Do the rules allow objectivity in choosing main entries? Or is the choice of main entry based on value judgments or arbitrary determination?

For several reasons, flowcharting is suggested as a method of analysis in order to answer these questions.

First, regarded as a "system," the rules lend themselves to study and evaluation through the techniques of systems analysis. Thus, flowcharting seems a suitable method of analysis for studying the logical sequence and relationships of the rules.

Second, accepting the idea that the rules form a system, flowcharting is a practical way of visualizing the system's component parts, showing, for instance, the language and structure of the rules and in what sequence they are arranged.

Third, as we indicated earlier, the designers of the *AACR* did not give consideration to computer applications. It is interesting, however, to study the rules with this view in mind—that is, to select a method of investigation that has implications for computer capabilities. All activities being considered for automation must be analyzed in terms of binary decisions. Generally speaking, if activities cannot be reduced to such decisions, then they cannot be programmed for the computer. Here again, flowcharting is a practical technique for analyzing the decision-making processes in that it represents the computer's logic.

By applying a flowcharting type of analysis to the *AACR* rules, it is possible to distinguish those operations which are clerical and amendable to computer processing from those which are intellectual and must be performed manually by humans.

Decision flowcharts provide an extremely detailed description of an operation or a set of operations, listing every decision and processing step that is made.[1] As Louis Schultheiss points out, decision flowcharts

> ... force the person making them to organize work on the basis of clear cut decisions with demonstrable and logical origins and results, and they force examination of the shadowy problem areas where no real decision has ever been made.[2]

While for this reason flowcharting proved itself to be very helpful in the investigation, it was, undeniably, a time-consuming technique. Developing the charts and revising them several times required a considerable effort. Some of the difficulties encountered stemmed from the flowcharting technique itself, others from the ambiguity and complexity of the rules. One difficulty was the lack of standardized procedures for flowcharting. For want of such procedures no two persons are likely to draw exactly the same flowchart to depict a given operation or process. One person, for instance, may be brief and cryptic, while another may show every detail in his flowchart.

To facilitate the presentation and understanding of the sample flowcharts presented in this study (Figures 7-11 below), it is necessary to state the particular procedures and conventions adopted.

    1. Conventional flowcharting symbols were used. The following IBM X20-8020 flowcharting template symbols were employed.

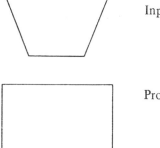

Input/output:
    Any type of data entered into or processed by the program

Processing:
    A group of program instructions which perform the processing function of the program

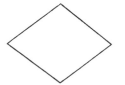

Decision:
    A point in the program where a decision must be made as to what action may be taken based upon stated conditions or questions

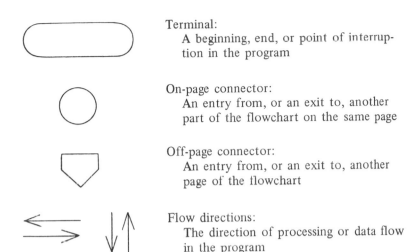

Terminal:
A beginning, end, or point of interruption in the program

On-page connector:
An entry from, or an exit to, another part of the flowchart on the same page

Off-page connector:
An entry from, or an exit to, another page of the flowchart

Flow directions:
The direction of processing or data flow in the program

2. Another convention used in the flowcharting was to make the descriptive statements within each symbol as brief as possible. This was not always easy to achieve. For one thing, the investigator avoided using his own terminology to prevent any distortion or interference with the logic of the rules. This seemed to be necessary as it is the purpose of the study to investigate the logic of the rules, not that of the author. Since the statements used in flowcharting follow, as exactly as possible, the wording of the rules, and since some of the wording used by the rules to describe processes or decisions is long and complex, brevity was not always possible.

3. An attempt was made to maintain a consistent depth of detail in all the charts. This was achieved simply by flowcharting every single detail given in each rule. Again, this was done to insure integrity in the interpretation of the rules.

4. To make the charts as clear as possible, each chart is presented along with a statement of the rule itself. The blocks on each chart are numbered in sequential order and these numbers are correlated with statements in the rule. This was done to help the reader study the charts in relation to the rules themselves.

5. To make the reading of the charts as smooth as possible, the graphic flow of processes in all the charts consistently follows one pattern. All the flow was made to go vertically from top to bottom.

6. A further convention generally used in flowcharting is that no directional flow lines are to be unconnected at any point. That is, every directional line should lead to another step in the chart. This convention could not always be followed. Because of the present organization of the rules, and because of their rather implicit style, many of the directional flow lines coming out of the decision blocks lead nowhere. Such flow lines are distinguished by

ending in an off-page connector with a question mark in the middle (see sample flowcharts, Figures 8 and 10). That some lines appear unconnected on a page of the flowchart does not mean, however, that they cannot, in actual fact, be connected. It would be possible to eliminate the unconnected flow lines either by directioning them into other steps or other rules, or by terminating them. Examples illustrating this are discussed in some detail in the analysis that follows.

Two other major problems inherent in the rules themselves caused difficulty in flowcharting. The first problem has to do with the organization of the rules, and the second is related to the language or wording of the rules. It would seem that if the rules were reorganized, the flow of decisions and processes would be smoother. For instance, many of the unconnected flow lines seem to be the result of poor organization, and they could probably be eliminated simply by reorganizing the rules. Although weaknesses in the organization of the rules will be pointed out in the analysis, for two reasons no attempt will be made to reorganize the rules. First, this would require a complete rewriting of the rules, which would be neither easy nor warranted. Second, as was pointed out earlier, the purpose of this investigation is to study the validity of the main entry principle, and to ascertain whether there is need for a set of rules for determinig main entry. From this point of view, any rewriting of the rules would be a waste of time.

The second problem is concerned with language and terminology. These affect the flow of decision lines to some extent, as will be shown later in the analysis. However, language and terminology have a more serious impact upon the degree of objectivity attainable in choosing entries according to the rules. Also the language problem causes many discrepancies and inconsistencies in the choice of entry and makes the separation of intellectual and clerical operations a difficult task.

A final point concerning the analysis in this chapter has to do with the number of rules studied. While in earlier chapters the number of rules analyzed was 129, in this chapter the number is increased to 145. The sixteen extra rules come about by considering as rules the preliminary notes and footnotes accompanying the 129 rules. While neither of these types of notes influences the determination of the entry or the assemblage of literary units, each affects the flow of decisions and processes and the movement from one rule to another. For this reason the notes were flowcharted as though they were rules by themselves. Although all rules were flowcharted, only a sample has been selected for presentation in this study to illustrate the problems encountered in using this technique.

The Analysis

The flowcharts were designed to show the steps in the decision-making process determined by the rules in relation to three major aspects: 1) the number of decisions and processes equired by each rule, 2) the flow of decisions from one rule to another and 3) the objectivity of the decision-making process in selecting main entries. This analysis seems to indicate that the rules for the choice of entry in *AACR* are a complex and disorganized system of procedures, the flow of the decisions is abrupt, and the decision-making process in determining main entries is subjective and based on value judgment.

Amount of Decision Making

The analysis of the flowcharts showed that the choice of entry according to Rules 1-32 of *AACR* is a complex and detailed decision-making process. The original thirty-two rules produced 145 flowcharts covering 156 pages. Each chart for a rule contained a sizable number of flowcharting blocks—i.e., decision, process, off-page connector, on-page connector, terminal and input blocks (see Figures 7-11). As was mentioned, off-page connectors are of two kinds. The first directs references to other rules which are indicated in the off-page connector block. The second, a block containing a question mark, indicates unconnected flow lines. In this part of the analysis only the first kind of off-page connector blocks and their influence on the number of decision-making steps is considered. Of course, the second kind of off-page connectors have a similar influence, that is, they have the effect of increasing the number of steps in the decision-making process. A detailed study of this latter kind will be given later in this chapter.

Table 12 provides a detailed analysis of the number and kinds of blocks required to program each rule. It also shows the number of unconnected decision flow lines. The 145 rules require, in all, 1,355 blocks with an average of 9.34 blocks per rule.

Decision blocks account for 879 of the total number with an average of 6.06 blocks per rule. The preliminary note to Rule 3 requires the largest number of decision blocks (27). There are eight rules for which only one decision block is necessary. These are 9B, 16B, 19B, 19B Exception 1, Footnote 21, 23B, 25C2, 29C and 30A.

Process blocks account for 393 of the total number of blocks, with an average of 2.71 per rule. The highest number of these blocks required for any rule is eleven blocks, illustrated by two rules, 29A and 25A1. Rules requiring only one process block in their flowcharting number thirty-two. As for off-page connectors, they total for all rules only eighty-three blocks, with an average of .57 per rule. The preliminary notes of Rules 3 and 20 are the rules with the largest number of off-page connectors, each having six. Of forty one rules, each has only one off-page connector. These represent a majority of the rules which refer to other rules.

An analysis of the flowcharts according to groups of rules, i.e., General Rules, Works with Authorship of Mixed Character, Certain Legal Publications, and Certain Religious Publications, is presented in Table 13. The figures in the table indicate that the average number of blocks per rule is comparable in the different groups. Rules for Certain Legal Publications have the highest average of 10.53 blocks per rule; followed by the General Rules, 9.30; rules for Certain Religious Publications, 9.25; and, finally, rules for Works with Authorship of Mixed Character, 8.32 blocks.

With regard to different kinds of blocks, there is considerable variation

103

TABLE 12

NUMBER AND KIND OF BLOCKS REQUIRED
IN THE FLOWCHARTING OF RULES 1-32 AND THEIR SUBRULES

Rule Number	No. of Decision Blocks Per Rule	No. of Processes Blocks Per Rule	No. of Off-Page Connectors Per Rule	Total No. of Blocks Per Rule	No. of Unconnected Decision Flow Lines Per Rule
1A	8	2	1	11	4
1B	5	2	0	7	4
2A	9	3	0	12	3
2B	5	4	0	9	3
2C	7	2	2	11	1
3PN	27	0	6	33	13
3A	5	4	0	9	2
3B1	2	2	0	4	2
3B1a	2	1	0	3	2
3B1b	3	2	0	5	2
3B1c	3	2	1	6	1
3B2	4	3	1	8	2
3C1	2	2	1	5	2
3C2	2	3	1	6	1
4PN	6	0	2	8	2
4A	6	4	0	10	2
5A	22	10	0	32	17
5A FN7	1	0	1	2	1
5B	15	5	2	22	8
6PN	3	1	0	4	3
6A	10	3	0	13	10
6B1	10	2	0	12	4
6B1 FN8	5	1	0	6	1
6B1 FN9	3	1	0	4	3
6B2	4	2	0	6	1
6C	2	1	0	3	2
6D1	10	2	0	12	5
6D1 FN11	3	1	1	5	1
6D2	4	2	0	6	3
7PN	11	1	2	14	4
7A	21	10	2	33	6
7B	12	5	1	18	8
7C	3	1	0	4	3
8A	5	4	0	9	2
8B	2	3	0	5	1
8C	4	4	0	8	3
8D1	6	1	0	7	4

TABLE 12 (cont'd.)

Rule Number	No. of Decision Blocks Per Rule	No. of Processes Blocks Per Rule	No. of Off-Page Connectors Per Rule	Total No. of Blocks Per Rule	No. of Unconnected Decision Flow Lines Per Rule
8D2	3	3	1	7	1
8E1	9	6	0	15	5
8E2	5	2	0	7	4
9A	10	2	0	12	2
9B	1	2	0	3	1
10	2	2	0	4	2
11PN	6	1	2	9	2
11PN FN15	1	1	0	2	1
11A	6	2	1	9	6
11B	7	2	1	10	7
11C	4	3	0	7	3
12	6	5	0	11	3
13A	7	3	0	10	2
13B	5	3	1	9	3
13C	4	3	0	7	3
14A	8	3	0	11	4
14A FN17	3	0	1	4	2
14B	2	2	0	4	2
15A	3	3	1	7	1
15B	2	1	1	4	2
16A	2	2	1	5	2
16B	1	1	0	2	1
17PN	6	0	0	6	5
17A1	18	5	0	23	7
17A2	10	1	0	11	2
17B	10	1	1	12	2
17C1a	4	2	3	9	4
17C1b	2	2	0	4	1
17C1c	2	1	0	3	2
17C2a	2	1	0	3	1
17C2b	5	2	2	9	2
17C2c	6	4	1	11	4
18A	3	3	0	6	1
18B	2	1	0	3	1
18C	4	6	0	10	1
18D	3	3	1	7	3
19PN	18	0	3	21	3
19A	12	1	2	15	7
19B	1	1	0	2	1
19B FN19	3	2	0	5	1

TABLE 12 (cont'd.)

Rule Number	No. of Decision Blocks Per Rule	No. of Processes Blocks Per Rule	No. of Off-Page Connectors Per Rule	Total No. of Blocks Per Rule	No. of Unconnected Decision Flow Lines Per Rule
19B Ex1	2	2	1	5	2
19B Ex1 FN2	1	1	1	3	1
19B Ex2	3	1	0	4	2
19B Ex3	3	1	0	4	3
20PN	15	0	6	21	1
20A	25	11	1	37	12
20B1	3	2	1	6	2
20B2	6	3	0	9	4
20C	4	3	1	8	2
20D	10	5	1	16	5
21A	5	2	0	7	4
21B	8	8	0	16	4
22A1	11	9	1	21	8
22A2	2	2	0	1	1
22B	7	1	0	8	3
22B Ex	2	2	0	4	1
22C	7	3	1	11	3
22D	6	3	1	10	2
23A	4	3	1	8	4
23B	1	1	0	2	1
23C	5	2	0	7	2
23D	8	2	0	10	6
23E	5	3	1	9	3
24A	15	2	1	18	5
24B	6	4	0	10	2
25A1	17	11	1	29	6
25A2a	13	7	2	22	6
25A2b	3	3	0	6	2
25B1	7	5	1	13	2
25B2	5	5	0	10	1
25C1	6	3	0	9	2
25C2	1	2	1	4	1
25D	3	2	0	5	2
25E1	6	5	0	11	2
25E2	4	2	0	6	1
25F1	5	3	2	10	3
25F2	4	4	1	9	3
25F3	2	2	0	4	2
25F4	5	2	2	9	2
26A1	6	3	0	9	4
26A2	5	6	0	11	3

TABLE 12 (cont'd.)

Rule Number	No. of Decision Blocks Per Rule	No. of Processes Blocks Per Rule	No. of Off-Page Connectors Per Rule	Total No. of Blocks Per Rule	No. of Unconnected Decision Flow Lines Per Rule
26B	6	5	0	11	1
26C1a(1)	10	9	0	19	5
26C1a(2)	3	1	0	4	1
26C1b	8	5	0	13	3
26C1c	6	4	0	10	1
26C1d	2	3	0	5	2
26C1e	2	3	0	5	2
26C1f	2	3	0	5	2
26C2a	5	3	0	8	3
26C2b	3	3	0	6	3
27A	5	3	1	9	4
27B	3	2	0	5	3
28	6	2	1	9	5
29A1	14	2	0	16	6
29A2	19	2	1	13	4
29A3	17	1	1	19	14
29B	6	2	0	8	2
29C	1	1	0	2	1
30A	1	1	1	3	1
30B	5	2	0	7	5
30C	3	1	1	5	3
31A	17	2	2	21	3
31A Ex	7	1	0	8	2
31B	8	3	0	11	5
32A	4	1	0	5	3
32B	5	2	0	7	1
TOTAL	879	393	83	1355	455

Abbreviations used:
    PN   Preliminary Note   FN   Footnote

from one group to another. Decision blocks are most numerous in Rules 27-32, followed by Rules 1-6, 20-26, and 7-19. As for process blocks, the largest number is found in Rules 20-26, followed by 7-29, 1-6 and 27-32. Off-page connectors are most numerous in Rules 1-6, the average being .63 per rule; in decreasing order are Rules 20-26, 27-32 and 7-19.

    Since a complete rule must be read in order to determine choice of

TABLE 13

NUMBER AND KINDS OF BLOCKS
IN THE FLOWCHARTING OF DIFFERENT GROUPS OF RULES

Rules	No. of Rules	Decisions		Processes		O.P. Con.		Total	
		No. of Blocks	Avg. Per Rule	No. of Blocks	Avg. Per Rule	No. of Blocks	Avg. Per Rule	No. of Blocks	Avg. Per Rule
General 1-6 & subrules	30	192	6.40	68	2.27	19	.63	279	9.30
Mixed Character 7-19 & subrules	52	281	5.40	122	2.34	20	.38	433	8.32
Legal Pub. 20-26 & subrules	47	294	6.25	175	3.72	26	.55	495	10.53
Religious Pub. 27-32 & subrules	16	112	7.00	28	1.75	8	.50	148	9.25
TOTAL	145	879	6.06	393	2.71	83	.57	1355	9.34

entry, it seems appropriate to summarize the average amount of decision making per rule. Table 14 shows this summary. As can be seen, on the average, a rule will contain 42.34 blocks, with a high of 147 in Rule 25 and a low of four in Rule 10. As to the kinds of blocks, Rule 25 has the largest number of both decision (81) and process (56) blocks, and shares, along with two other rules—3 and 20—the largest number of off-page connectors (10).

TABLE 14

NUMBER OF DECISION, PROCESS AND OFF-PAGE
CONNECTOR BLOCKS IN THE FLOWCHARTING OF RULES 1-32

	Number of Blocks	Average Per Rule	High	Low
Decisions	879	27.47	81	2
Process	393	12.28	56	2
Off-Page Connectors	83	2.59	10	0
TOTAL	1355	42.34	147	4

The above analysis supports the fact that the choice of entry according to Rules 1-32 of *AACR* is a complex decision-making process. Moreover, the many steps in this process are further increased when one considers that any given rule may incorporate references to other rules. Before making a final choice for the main entry, any of the rules referred to must be consulted, thus increasing the number of decision steps doubly or triply, depending on the number of the references as well as their specificity. The ramifications of these references on the flow of decision are discussed in detail later in this chapter.

It must be remembered that the determination of the main entry is only one aspect of the descriptive cataloging process. Choice of entry is usually accompanied by other determinations such as the choice of the added entries, the forms of the headings and the description of the item in hand. Each of these determinations may be supposed to involve an equal or larger number of decision-making steps, depending upon the various rules specified for them. In other words, the complexity lies not in the choice of main entry alone; it also permeates the descriptive cataloging process as a whole.

The complexity of the rules for choice of entry in *AACR* stems not only from the fact that the rules are overlong but also from their excessive concern with the treatment of special types of publications. These are the same reasons that subjected the ALA 1949 rules to criticism and eventually led to their revision. In attempting to correlate the rules for choice of entry in *AACR* with those in ALA 1949, F. Bernice Field showed that the thirty-two rules in the former correspond to thirty-eight complete rules and twenty-one subrules in the latter.[3] From another point of view, considering each of the subrules, footnotes, and preliminary notes as separate rules, the 149 rules of the *AACR* can be said to correspond to 211 in ALA 1949. Although with the new *AACR* there has been a considerable decrease in the actual number of rules, the text of the rules does not seem to have been correspondingly reduced. For instance, in comparing the text of Rules 7, 8, 11, 14 and 15 of *AACR* with the corresponding rules in ALA, the author found that, in several cases, the text of the rules in *AACR* is longer. This expansion of text in the *AACR* rules seems to have resulted from the practice of including in one rule provisions that were scattered in ALA under several rules. Thus, the reduction in the number of the rules in *AACR* is offset by the enlarging of the text of the rules. In the introductory matter of the *AACR* it is indicated that the text of the new rules for both choice of entry and form of heading are less extensive by one-fifth than the corresponding rules in the 1949 edition.[4] Not indicated, however, is precisely the extent to which the rules for choice of entry alone were reduced.

With regard to specifying rules for special types of publications, the *AACR* is not different from the ALA 1949. With the exception of the first four rules, the thirty-two rules are devoted to certain types of publications. Rules 5-6 and 19-32 are explicitly designed as such. For example, Rule 5 is for "collections," 6 for "serials," 19 for "related works," 20-26 for "certain legal publications," and 27-32 are for "certain religious publications." As for Rules 7-18, they also are for the treatment of certain types of publications;

however, this is disguised by the fact that the rules appear under labels denoting conditions of authorship. For example, Rule 7 is called "adapter or original author," 8 "artist or author of text," 11 "commentator or author," 14 "reviser or original author," 15 "translator or author." The corresponding rules in ALA 1949 were labeled "adaptations," "works of art," "commentaries," "revisions," and "translations."

As for Rules 17 and 18, the first is both for the treatment of special types of publications (e.g., government and official) and for types of authorship (e.g., chiefs of state and heads of governments). Rule 18, on the other hand, deals with the choice between a parent body and a subordinate unit and is by nature more related to rules for form of heading than to rules for choice of entry. The rule can be considered out of place where it stands; more logically, it could have been incorporated in Chapter 3.

It could be said that the only real or effective difference between *AACR* and ALA 1949 is that the first has, with some exceptions, separated choice of entry from construction of headings. Choice of entry is treated in Chapter 1, and the form or construction of headings is treated in Chapters 2 to 4. Some of the exceptions to this are Rules 3C, 6D, 18 and those of Rules 20-32 which are concerned with form headings. In ALA 1949 the two problems of entry choice and heading construction are not separated.

As the present study intends to show, the need for such an involved and complicated decision-making process for selecting main entries is questionable, especially in light of present developments in library technology. Why do we need to select a main entry? It is known that:

1. Even when an author's name appears on the title page of a publication, the rules do not always permit an author main entry, thus disregarding the principle of intellectual responsibility.
2. The rules do not always provide the author entries necessary for assembling literary units, thus disregarding one of the stated basic functions of the catalog.
3. The rules designed for choosing main entries are illogically structured, which results in arbitrary choices and in many inconsistencies (this will be discussed later in more detail).
4. The main entry is only one of the various access points that a user might seek or know of in approaching the catalog. In multiple entry catalogs, the main entry is quite often disregarded and even the new ALA filing rules provide a rule which bypasses the main entry in filing added entries. In one-entry catalogs, those in which there are no added entries, there are many difficulties in finding the information wanted.
5. With the present state of technology neither the main entry nor the complete form of heading is necessary for the retrieval of information. Any entry is considered as only one among the various labels that can be used in identifying a publication. Moreover, as was seen earlier, current studies show truncated entries are successfully used in retrieving information from large files.

Flow of Decisions

The complexity of the decision-making process in the selection of main entries is further detected through an analysis of the flow charts in terms of the flow of decision. The flow charts make it clear that in many cases the flow of decision within a rule, or from one rule to another, is inconsistent and abrupt.

In the discussion of methodology, it was pointed out that many of the decision flow lines are unconnected. Table 12 above shows that a total of 454 flow lines were unconnected, with an average of 3.04 per rule. Rule 5A ranked highest as it contained seventeen unconnected flow lines. On the other hand, twenty-four rules had only one unconnected flow line each.

On the charts these unconnected flow lines are distinguished by off-page connector symbols with a question mark in the middle (see Figures 8 and 10). The existence of such unconnected flow lines means that a rule does not itself allow the choice of the main entry and also that it fails to lead the reader to another rule which might make such a choice possible. Hence, the reader who does not possess a fairly good knowledge of the rules will be forced to go back and forth between the rules, the table of contents, the introduction, and the index to find a pertinent rule. This naturally consumes a great deal of time, making the choice of entry a difficult task.

Since unconnected flow lines are an unacceptable practice in flow-charting, an attempt was made to connect or terminate them whenever possible. This process required examining each of these lines in relation to the other parts of the rule, and/or to the preceding or succeeding rules. Because of the complexity of this process and time limitations, however, the investigator was forced to end his efforts with Rule 4. The analysis thus was limited to sixteen rules containing forty-six unconnected flow lines. Out of these forty-six lines, thirty-five could be connected by making references to other rules that were thought as the next logical step. The remaining eleven unconnected flow lines were terminated, since it was felt that this was the only next logical step. An example of a terminal ending of an unconnected directional flow line is shown on the modified flowchart for Rule 4A shown in Figure 7. Decision block number 7 concerns whether or not authors are named on the title page. The "yes" flow line leads to a solution, which is to make an added entry for the author named first. The "no" flow line, however, ends in a terminal since there is nothing to be done in the case where no author is named on the title page.

This analysis shows that unconnected flow lines result from two major causes: 1) the illogical organization and structure of the rules, and 2) the inadequacy and inconsistency of the directional references provided by the rules.

1. Organization and Structure of the Rules

Examination of only a few of the flow charts, those for Rules 1-4, discloses several problems in the organizing and the sequencing of the rules.

On the chart for Rule 1A (Figure 8), block number 1 is for the decision of whether or not a work is of a single authorship. The "yes" flow line leads to the next step. The "no" flow line, however, is unconnected. Upon

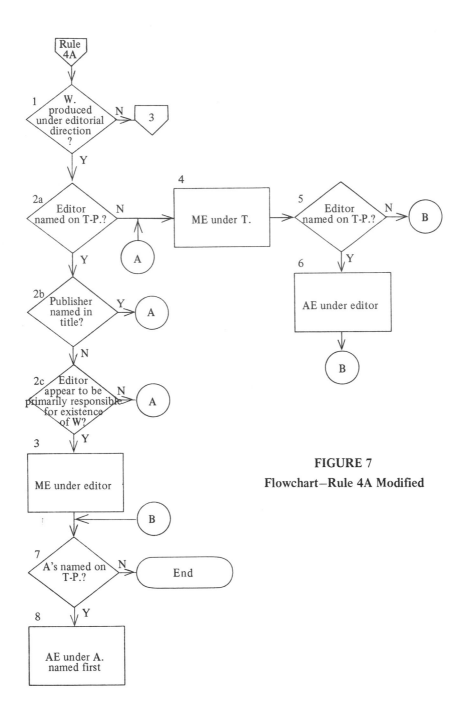

FIGURE 7

Flowchart—Rule 4A Modified

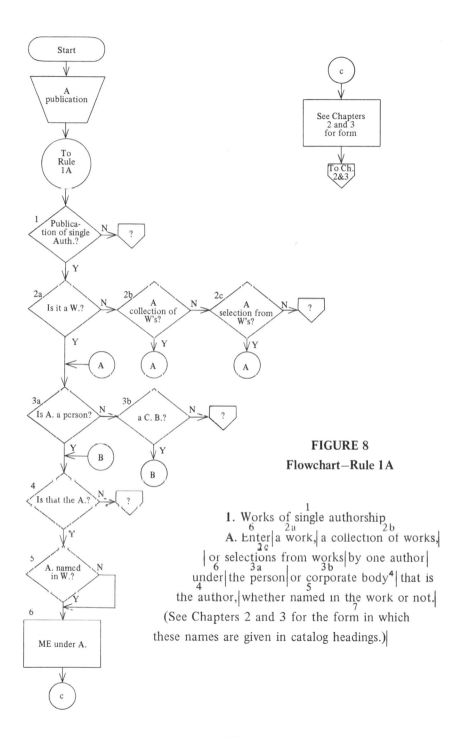

FIGURE 8

Flowchart—Rule 1A

1. Works of single authorship[1]
   A. Enter[6] a work,[2a] a collection of works,[2b] or selections from works[2c] by one author[6] under[3a] the person[6] or corporate body[4][3b] that is the author,[4] whether named in the work or not.[5] [7] (See Chapters 2 and 3 for the form in which these names are given in catalog headings.)

113

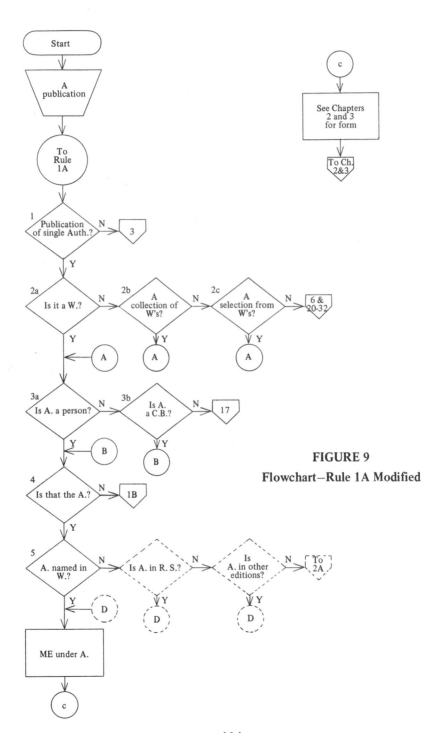

FIGURE 9

Flowchart—Rule 1A Modified

studying this line it was connected with Rule 3 as shown in Figure 9. The reason for the lack of connection is that the rules are not logically organized. The principles underlying the rules for entry follow a prescribed order:

1) Entry should be under author or principal author when one can be determined.
2) Entry should be under editor when there is no author or principal author and when the editor is primarily responsible for the existence of the work.
3) Entry should be under a compiler named on the title page in the case of collections of works by various authors.
4) Entry should be under title in the case of other works whose authorship is diffuse, indeterminate, or unknown.[5]

The rules, however, follow a different order or arrangement. Rule 1 is for "works of single authorship," Rule 2 deals with "works of unknown or uncertain authorship . . .," Rule 3 is for "works of shared authorship," and Rule 4 is called "works produced under editorial direction." This order of arrangement differs from the order in which the principles are arranged and is less logical. For instance, Rule 2 for works of unknown authorship is inserted between several rules for *known* authorship. Rule 1 is for *known* single authorship and Rules 3-5 are for *known* shared authorship, editorship, or compilership. Rule 2, therefore, interrupts the logical sequence of several rules common in nature. Thus, as is shown on the chart, the decision flow is interrupted. From this point of view, the insertion of Rule 2 between Rules 1 and 3 is illogical and out of order. Another problem is caused by this organizational deficiency, namely a duplication and repitition of the rules that increases unnecessarily the size and body of the Code. For instance, Rule 3B1c is a repetition of Rule 2. Rule 2 is for unknown, uncertain . . . authorship and is not limited to any number of unknown authors, as is Rule 3B1c. The latter rule could have been eliminated if all of the rules for known authorship were grouped together in one sequence, and if Rule 2 were placed at the end of the sequence, with references to it from all the other rules as appropriate.

Similar organizational problems are evident in other rules, such as Rule 3. On the chart for Rule 3B1 (see Figure 10), decision block number 1 concerns whether or not a work is by principal author. The "yes" directional flow line leaves the decision block unconnected. However, it can be easily connected simply by referring it back to Rule 3A that deals with works which have primary authorship responsibility. This reference (see Figure 11) is done by assumption, since the reader of the rules will read Rule 3A first. And, thus, he will be able to recognize this fact once he reads through Rule 3B1. On the other hand, decision block number 2 concerns whether or not the authors are more than three. The "no" directional flow line leads to entering the work under the first-named author since the authors are not more than three. The "yes" directional flow line—i.e., the authors are more than three—is, however, unconnected. The reason for this lack of connection is the illogical separation of Rule 3B1 from Rule 3B2, which provides for the entry

115

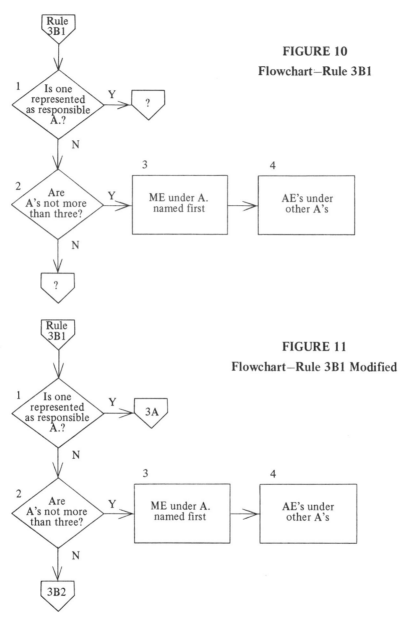

FIGURE 10

Flowchart—Rule 3B1

FIGURE 11

Flowchart—Rule 3B1 Modified

B. Principal author not indicated

1. If no[1] one is represented as principal author[2] and if there are not[3] more than three authors,[3] enter under the one that is named first[4] and make added entries under the others.[4]

116

in the case where there are more than three authors. Rule 3B1 itself does not make any provision in this case, nor does it refer to another rule that provides an answer to this question. It is not until the reader reaches Rule 3B2 that the answer is found: main entry is prescribed under title with an added entry under the first-named author. In other words, it is only on coming across Rule 3B2 that one discovers that the direction of the "yes" flow line from decision block number 2 is to Rule 3B2, as shown in Figure 11. The separation of Rules 3B1 and 3B2 seems uncalled for and impractical.

Between Rules 3B1 and 3B2 there are three other subrules. The first is for works in more than one volume, the second is for works in more than one edition, and the third deals with unknown authorship. The latter, as was mentioned earlier, is a repetition of Rule 2. As for the first two subrules, they should not be listed as subrules to 3B1 only. Their provisions apply to 3A as well as to 3B1. Many authors, while appearing as principal authors on one volume or one edition of a work, become secondary in responsibility on later volumes or editions of the work. These two subrules more logically might have been listed as Rule 3C and 3D. However, it can even be asked why these two rules should exist. As stated earlier in Chapter II, the selection of main entry on the basis of their provisions is illogical and biased. Determination of main entry is not based on primary responsibility nor is it based on the order of the authors on the title page of the volume in hand. Lubetzky recommended that for this case the more practical solution is to make main entry under the title.

2. Directional References

Like the organization and structure of the rules, directional references are essential for smoothing out the flow of decisions from one rule to another. Here again the flowcharting of the rules helps to show that the flow of decisions in some cases is aborted because of inadequate directional references. An analysis of the directional references will help illustrate this problem.

The 149 rules flowcharted contained eighty-three directional references. Directional references are represented on the flowcharts by off-page connector symbols with the number of the rules referred to inserted in the middle of the symbol (see Figures 7-11). Table 15 shows the distribution of these references classified according to type of rules referred to, i.e., rules for choice of entry, choice of form of heading and description.

As can be seen from the table, of the 149 rules flowcharted, only fifty-eight make references to other rules. Also it is clear that not all of the references are to rules for the choice of entry. Of the eighty-three references, twenty-five are to rules either for choice of form of heading or for description. Only fifty-eight or 69.8 percent of the references are to rules for choice of entry.

As to the number of references given by each rule, only a few—nine rules—give more than one reference. Two rules, 3PN and 20PN, give six references each; one rule gives three references; and six rules give two references each. Of the remaining fifty rules, thirty make one reference each and twenty do not give any reference at all. Some of the rules not making any

117

TABLE 15
DIRECTIONAL REFERENCES
DISTRIBUTED ACCORDING TO TYPES OF RULES REFERRED TO

No. of Rules	No. of Referencing Rules	Number of References to					
		Rules for Entry		Rules for Form		Rules for Descrip.	
		No. of Ref.	%	No. of Ref.	%	No. of Ref.	%
149	58	58	69.87	21	25.30	4	4.81

references are responsible for breaks in the decision flow. For instance, the flowchart for Rule 1A (see figure 8 above) shows that there is a break in the flow of the "no" directional lines emanating from decision blocks number 1, 2c, 3b, and 4. As these lines were studied, they were connected as shown on the chart in Figure 9. The causes for the breaking are several. The first line is the "no" flow line off decision block number 1. It was connected by referring it to Rule 3. As was shown earlier, it is broken because there is in Rule 1A no reference to Rule 3, which is for shared authorship or works of multiple authorship. The second broken line emanates from decision block number 2c. This line was referred to Rule 6C. It results from the fact that there are some types of publications by personal authors which are treated under rules other than 1A, but the rule fails to make mention of this fact. Rule 6C for serials by a personal author might have been mentioned. Rule 1A, while properly not concerned with serials, might at least have directed the reader to rules covering such works. Similarly, the third unconnected line, the "no" flow line leaving decision block number 3B, was connected by referring it to Rule 17. This is due to the fact that the rule fails to mention the case which arises when a choice must be made between a personal author and a corporate body. It is quite common that a publication will have a single personal author noted on the title page, but this publication might belong to a corporate body also noted on the title page. In this case the publication might be treated according to the provisions of Rule 17. Rule 1A, however, fails to make this fact clear—that is, it fails to refer the reader to Rule 17, which is concerned with the choice between a corporate body and a personal author. Such reference is recognized as important by both Rules 3 and 4 and is given in their preliminary notes.

Connecting the last line was more obvious than the above three. This line emanating from block 4 was linked with Rule 1B, because it was assumed that if there is an author named on the title page who is not the author, then he falls within the category of fictitious or erroneous authors and thus should be referred to Rule 1B.

These problems and similar ones are due not only to lack of references, but also to the lack of preliminary or scope notes and the inconsistent handling of such notes in the rules. Although notes play a major role in directing the flow of decisions and in showing the scope of the rules, they are not used particularly effectively in the rules. Of the nine rules which contain more than one directional reference, five are in the form of preliminary notes (PN). Table 16 groups rules which provide directional references and shows references according to the type of rules referred to. As can be seen from the table, the PNs tend to be rules incorporating a number of references. PNs of Rules 3 and 20, for instance, each incorporate six references.

PN of Rule 19 makes four references and the PNs for Rule 4 and for Rule 7-18 make two references each. In general, the total number of references incorporated in the PNs is twenty, or 34.4 percent of the total number of references made for the choice of entry. This fact is an indication of the importance of PNs in directing the flow of decisions through the rules. However, the completeness of the references given by the PNs varied greatly. While Rule 20PN makes reference to almost all of the rules (five out of six) for certain legal publications, the PN for Rules 7-17 makes no reference to any of the Rules 7-17 but refers only to Rules 2A and 2C. The reader therefore has to examine each of these eleven rules individually whenever he has a publication which might be covered by one of these rules.

In some other classes where PNs are needed they are not given at all. For instance, many of the problems relating to Rule 1 discussed earlier could be resolved by adding a PN directing the reader to other pertinent rules. Similarly, a PN for Rule 5 seems necessary. Seven rules have references to Rule 5. It is likely that some of these rules could well be eliminated from the code if a PN were made for Rule 5. For instance, Rule 15B states: "treat a collection of translations of works by different authors under the rule for collections (see Rule 5)."[6] Also, Rule 25F4 reads: "Enter any other collection of agreements between countries, states, intergovernmental bodies, etc., under the provisions of Rule 5, if monographic. . . ."[7] If a scope note were made for Rule 5 listing all such collections that could be treated under it, the rules making such references could be eliminated from the code, thus reducing the size of its text and some of its complexity.

In examining the fifty-eight directional references to the rules for choice of entry, it was found that they vary considerably in specificity (see Table 16). Some are specific references from one subrule to another. For example, Rule 5B refers to Rule 5A. Others are general references—that is, they are from a subrule to a general rule. For instance, Rule 13B refers to Rule 3. Another group of references is very broad in that they are made from one rule to a group of rules. For instance, Rule 29A3 refers to Rules 1-5 and Rule 11A refers to the "General Rules." In such cases the determination of the main entry is a rather complex and time-consuming problem. The reader must examine several rules before making a decision, which requires a considerable amount of time.

What is shown by the above analysis is that the use of directional flow lines in the rules is inconsistent and, in some cases, aborted. Moreover, preliminary notes, which serve a primary purpose in directing the flow of decisions and in showing the scope of a rule or a group of rules, are not used

TABLE 16
DIRECTIONAL REFERENCES

Rule Number	Entry	Reference to Form of Heading	Description
1A		Chap. 2 & 3	
2C		33J, 51A-D	
3PN	4,5,8A,13,16,17		
3B1c	3A		
3B2	4		
3C1		121B1	
3C2	3A		
4PN	6,17		
5A FN7	205-206		
5B	5A	103	
6D1 FN11	14		167K
PN 7-18	2A,2C		
7A	14A, 15		
7B		102C3	
8D2	5		
11PN	24B		
11A	1-5		
11B	1-5		
13B	3		
14A FN17	7A		
15A	7		
15B	5		
16A	13C		
17B	17A		
17C1a	17C2,20A	80	
17C2c		80	
18D		69	
19 PN	7,14,15		
19A			155
19A3			168
19B Ex,FN21	19B		
19B Ex1			243D
20 PN	20,21,22,23,24,25		
20A		80A	
21B1	20A		
20C		81	
20D	5		
22A1		80A	

120

TABLE 16 (cont'd.)

Rule Number	Reference to		
	Entry	Form of Heading	Description
22C	20C		
22D		106	
23A		83	
23E	23D		
24A	24B		
25A1	25A2		
25A2a	25A1	87-99	
25B1	25A1		
25C2	25C1		
25F1	25A1,25B1		
25F2	25A1		
25F4	5,6		
27A		108-118	
28		Chap. 4	
29A2		109El	
29A3	General Rules		
30A		92	
30C	5		
31A	94,95A		

to full effect. Consequently, the text of the rules is unnecessarily large and the flow of the decision-making process in selecting main entries is obscured. As a result, choosing a main entry requires much effort from the cataloger, in that he must examine several rules in the course of reaching a decision. Is this a logical procedure—especially since many of the decisions reached are arbitrary in nature and do not necessarily reflect authorship responsibility, supposedly a primary objective of the rules? The subjectivity involved in the choice of main entry is discussed in the following part of this analysis.

Objectivity in Selecting Main Entries

It has just been shown that certain language problems complicate the flowcharting process. The language of the rules affects also the objectivity with which main entries are determined. Upon close examination of the rules it becomes evident that the determination of main and added entries is not based on principles, nor is it a result of an objective decision-making process. Many of the choices suggested by the rules are arbitrary in that the rules embody subjective phrases, that is, phrases widely open to individual interpretation and value judgment. This results in inconsistent decisions and discrepancies in the choice of entries. Probably the most obvious illustrations of these value judgment phrases are "in case of doubt" and "if there is doubt." These two phrases are used in eight rules: 6B2, 8A, 8E2, 9A, 11C, 17C1, 17B and 24B. Phrases like these make the choice of entry a guessing game. Whenever a cataloger wishes to escape from making a decision, he can enter the publication under one entry or another and justify his action by the fact that he was in doubt. Determining main and added entries in such a manner is certainly arbitrary and should not be permitted by a logical set of cataloging rules.

The most commonly used subjective phrases in the rules are grouped in the following list:

1. Whether named in work or not
2. If named on title page
3. If openly named
4. If openly named in work
5. Appears openly on the work
6. If known
7. If there are no more than three authors
8. Named first author
9. Appears first on the title page
10. Named in any edition
11. Named first in the first edition
12. Attributed in editions of the work
13. Named first on the title page of the first volume
14. Principal responsibility
15. Reference sources
16. Author given greater prominence by wording or typography
17. Consensus of scholarly opinion
18. Author whose heading is first in alphabetical order
19. That is the author
20. Preferably in English
21. Formal history
22. Home country, i.e., country of library for which cataloging is done
23. Enter according to the following order of preference
24. Written specially for the same occasion or for publication in hand
25. Noteworthy feature
26. Important feature
27. If for any reason
28. Material is principle element
29. Material is minor element

Choice of entry according to the phrases listed above is in no way guided by an objective determination of authorship responsibility. To emphasize the point that the subjectivity implied in such phrases complicates the choice of entry and results in many inconsistencies and contradictions, some specific illustrations will now be considered and examined in more detail.

The first illustration deals with the first phrase on the above list, "whether named in the work or not." This phrase is used only in Rule 1A and can perhaps be considered one of the most perplexing, contradictory and ambiguous phrases. Rule 1A requests that the main entry be made under the author of the work "whether" he is "named in the work or not." A general reader or an untrained cataloger would probably wonder about such a requirement. How can a work be entered under its author if no author is personally named in any part of the work? Actually, in drawing the flowchart for Rule 1A, this phrase presented a problem as it resulted in an unacceptable loop (see Figure 8). As shown in the chart, both the "yes" and "no" decision flow lines emanating from the decision block number 5 containing this phrase end with the same process. Logically this should not happen, and some other steps must take place before the "no" decision line can be correctly directed. Actually, this phrase calls for checking reference sources or other editions of the work in order to establish the main entry when the author is not named on the title page. This means the flowchart as shown in Figure 9 must be modified. However, this might be understandable only to the experienced or initiated cataloger. In no place in the rule is there mention of the process required to establish the main entry. Rules 2 and 3, however, explicitly state this process. Probably the only clue to the meaning of the statement in Rule 1A is in the second example given under the rule. This example reads:

> *Title page:*
> De Bello Germanico . . . written in 1918 by the author
> of Undertones of War
> *Main entry under the author of* Undertones of War,
> *Edmund Blunden*

As can be implied from the example, the cataloger searched in some reference tool, i.e., card catalog, NUC, etc., to establish the name of the author of the book *Undertones of War*. This name was then used as the main entry for the book in question, *De Bello Germanico*. Again, the process of searching reference sources for determining the main entry in this case is not described explicitly by the rule. It is only implicitly suggested by example and left to individual decision. This type of ambiguity in the rules makes their use difficult and their interpretation the business of only the experienced cataloger.

Entering a work under its author "whether named in the work or not" is another case where subjectivity of judgment is unavoidable. Compare, for instance, the treatment of the book *De Bello Germanico* with the treatment of works of unknown authorship in general (Rule 2). By Rule 2C the main entry for the book entitled *The Unveiled Heart, A Simple Story by the Author of Early Impressions* is recommended under its title and an added entry is prescribed under the "form of the phrase indicating the author," i.e., Early Impressions, Author of. The justification for this different treatment of *De Bello Germanico* and *The Unveiled Heart* is that for the latter the author is unknown.

Generally the determination of the main entry with respect to whether the author is known is usually a function of one or a combination of three possibilities: 1) the availability of another work by the author in the library's collection, 2) the availability of adequate reference sources, and 3) the cataloger's knowledge of a given author and his works. Any one or all of these factors may contribute to establishing the identity of the author. The first two are dependent on the size of the library and its financial condition. The smaller the library, the less chance there is that it possesses additional works by a given author. Also, the smaller the library the less chance there is that adequate reference sources are available. Smaller libraries usually have smaller collections and cannot afford to acquire expensive reference sources. They are thus at a disadvantage in determining this kind of author entry. There is clearly opportunity for subjective decision making, with the consequence being inconsistency in making entries. That is, different libraries may enter the same work under different entries. The determination of the main entry, then, appears in cases such as these to be dependent on who is cataloging the book, where, and what tools he has.

Erroneous and fictitious authors present a similar problem, especially when they are not so indicated on the title page or in any other part of the publication. This case has more dire consequences. If the cataloger cannot establish the identity of the author, the end result is that the publication is entered under the erroneous or fictitious author. Actually, Rule 1B does not consider this possibility at all.

The problems which arise in determining "unknown," "erroneous," or "fictitious" authors are further intensified in the case of foreign publications. The size of the library is not of much help in this regard inasmuch as what is required are 1) foreign reference sources, which are usually rare or non-existent, and 2) catalogers equipped with foreign languages as well as knowledge of the history, culture, literature, etc., of the particular country. Catalogers of this type are scarce, even in large libraries.

According to the rules, then, the practice of entering a book under the author "whether named in the work or not" is applicable only in the case of main entries. When an author is to be used as an added entry, a provision such as "if openly named," "appears openly on the work," or "if named on the title page" is made. An illustration of the discrimination between authors on the basis of type of entry can be drawn from Rule 16A. The rule states:

> Enter a work written by one person for another person in whose name it is presented under the latter person, with an added entry under the person who did the writing if his name appears openly in the work.[8]

Obviously, the examples under the rules follow the rules' provisions. The second example under the rules, for instance, reads:

> *Title page:*
> A narrative of the adventures and suffering of John
> R. Jewitt, only survivor of the crew of the ship Boston
> (*Written by Richard Alsop as though in the words of Jewitt...*)

This example recommends the *"main entry under Jewitt"* and requires no added entry under Alsop because he is *not named in the work.*

Similarly, Rule 4A recommends for some cases a main entry under title and an added entry under editor "if he is named on the title page." The results of such prescriptions are shown in the following two examples given under the rule:

> *Title page:*
> A new survey of universal knowledge//
> Encyclopedia Britannica
> > (*Editor's preface signed John V. Dodge,*
> > *executive editor; Howard E. Kasch, man-*
> > *aging editor*)

> *Title page:*
> Larousse de la musique; publié sous la direc-
> tion de Norbert Defourcq avec la collaboration
> de Félix Raugel [et] Armand Machabey, Paris,
> Larousse, 1957.
> *Added entry under Defourcq.*

These two examples not only show the different treatment of authors depending on whether they are considered as main or added entries, but also the different treatment they receive when being considered for the added entry.

The main point the examples serve to illustrate, however, is that determination of authorship according to the rules seems important in some cases but not in others; it seems important when the main entry is in question but not when added entries are considered.

Phrase number six on the above list, "if there are not more than three authors," is another illustration of the subjectivity permitted by the rules. The so-called "rule of three"[9] is used consistently throughout the rules for making main and added entries. In the case of main entries the rules, such as Rule 3B1, require that "if there are not more than three authors" the main entry is to be "under the one named first" and added entries are to be made under the other authors. If there are more than three authors, however, Rule 3B2 recommends main entry under title and an added entry for the first-named author on the title page. Similarly, in the case of added entries many of the rules require an added entry under the first-named author if there are more than three. One wonders why the figure three has been established as a decision point deviding two different choices of entries. Lubetzky points out that this is a matter of tradition. This type of tradition, however, is both detrimental to the construction of a logical code and unfair to authors. It is detrimental because, as was pointed out earlier, it complicates decision-making processes and unnecessarily increases the size of the code to provide for works published in different editions and works published in more than one volume where the order of the authors on the title pages might differ. The tradition is unfair because while the relation of each author to a book may be the same and the intellectual responsibility may be equally shared among the three authors, the rules single out or favor only one of them and place him in a more responsible position.

Another illustration of inconsistencies and confusion resulting from the language of the rules can be drawn from Rules 1 and 2. In these two rules alone, nine terms are used for distinguishing different types of authors.

	Term	Rule Number
1	Erroneous	1B, 2A Example 3
2	Fictitious	1B
3	Unknown	2A, 2C Example 4
4	Uncertain	2A, 2B Example 1
5	Attributed	2A, 2A Example 2, 2B
6	Possible	2A Example 3
7	Probable	2B
8	Generally attributed	2B Example 1
9	Real	1B

The above nine terms as used in Rules 1 and 2 need definition and explanation. Some of these terms are used in more than one of the subrules under Rules 1 and 2. In some cases, however, it can happen that the meaning of a term differs according to the subrule in which it is used. In some other cases, two different terms are used by two subrules or by the same subrule as synonyms. A few examples will serve to illustrate some of the cases of this inconsistency and ambiguity.

Although the terms "uncertain," "attributed," "possible," "probable" and "generally attributed" all indicate some degree of doubt as to the identity of the author, the rules distinguish between them in prescribing main and added entries. Only in the cases of "probable" and "generally attributed" authors do the rules suggest main entry under the author. (Incidentally, the two terms are used by Rule 2B more or less as synonymous.) In all the other cases of doubt the rules recommend main entry under the title. The implication is that the rules require searching reference sources and other editions of the work only to ascertain a degree of doubt and then on the basis of this the determination of the main entry is made. It can be asked if this is worth time and effort. Why not treat all doubtful authors on an equal basis and enter their works under the title?

Also on the added entry level discrepancies can be found. First, attributed authors are treated differently in Rules 2A and 2B. Rule 2A requires added entries for this type of author; Rule 2B, however, recommends only author-title references. Also, in the first rule the number of added entries is limited to three, while in the second no limit is put on the number of references permitted.

Another example is the case of "erroneous" authors. Both Rule 1B and Example 3 under Rule 2A require an added entry under an erroneous author. Rule 1B, in particular, demands that this author be a "real" person. Yet we find Rule 13C prescribing an added entry under a "spirit." Is a spirit a real person?

126

The Computer and the Rules

As was pointed out earlier, the *AACR* has been criticized for its disregard of the new technology and possible computer applications. Inasmuch as computerized descriptive cataloging has been predicted for the foreseeable future, it seems appropriate to conclude this chapter by discussing the implications of its findings in relation to computerized operations. The direction of the discussion will be towards answering the following questions: Is it feasible to program the rules for the choice of entry in *AACR* to be used on the computer for the selection of main entries? Is it desirable or necessary to have the rules programmed for computerized cataloging?

While the analysis has shown that the decision processes embodied in the rules can be flowcharted in a general schematic fashion, it is obvious that programming the rules as they now stand is not feasible, because the choice of the main entry according to the rules is an intellectual process. This process involves the making of judgments as well as searching in reference sources, in other editions of a given work, etc. The computer, on the other hand, is only an electronic device which accepts the data it is given and processes it according to prescribed instructions. Computers are not capable of making judgments or decisions. For instance, they cannot make a choice on the basis of doubt or principal responsibility. They are not capable of deciding whether or not the illustrations in a given work are an important feature, or whether or not a commentary is a minor or the major part of a work. Computers cannot distinguish between a collection and a work produced under editorial direction. Nor can they decide whether or not a work is an expression of a corporate thought or an expression of a personal author. Finally, computers cannot determine whether the author of a work is mentioned in any part of it, when the name is not explicitly given on the title page. These are only a few examples of the many intellectual decisions that must be made by humans individually in the course of cataloging a book. The computer cannot assist in such decisions.

Similarly, the computer could be of little assistance in determining the main entries from reference sources. Conceivably one of two methods could be employed. Either reference sources could be stored in computer memory and a program written to search them when necessary, or the searching of reference sources could be done manually and the information input to the computer for final processing.

Obviously, the first method is impractical and probably impossible. From the point of view of storage capability, a file of information composed of all reference sources used by catalogers to establish main entries would be prohibitively expensive. As for the second method, human interference would be required, which would devalue the use of having the rules fed to the computer in the first place. It would be much easier and probably faster if all the processes leading to the choice of entry were done manually.

Another point brought out by the above analysis is that the rules are overlong and complex. Converting them into machine readable format would be an extremely complex and difficult task. The resulting programs would be inordinately long, cumbersome and, in short, too inefficient to make computer processing economically feasible.

Again, from another point of view, converting the rules for choice of entry into machine-readable form is undesirable. It is commonly known that in present computerized catalogs the main entry serves little if any purpose. The impossibility of standardizing main entries, as would be required for computer applications, has been recognized by the library profession. This can be seen in the adoption of the International Standard Bibliographic Description, designed for the purpose of transferring bibliographic information stored on computer data bases. In Chapter II of this investigation, it was also pointed out that in a computerized catalog the main entry is only one of the various tags a patron might use for retrieving a bibliographic record.

As the computerized catalogs gain more popularity and are more employed in libraries, even the question of the correct or complete form of heading might become merely theoretical. Present experiments with computerized systems such as the SPIRES/BALLOTS Project and the Ohio College Library Center have shown that truncated entries for authors and/or titles can be used efficiently for retrieving bibliographic records from large data files. When the objective is the production by computer of traditional bibliographic tools such as book catalogs, bibliographies, and catalog cards, again the main entry is not important. The computer can be programmed to sort records in a file according to any order desired—for instance, by author, title, or subject. In other words, with the rapidly advancing computer technology, the question of the main entry is only a theoretical one, and programming the rules for its choice is niether a simple process nor a warranted one.

FOOTNOTES

[1] Paul J. Fasana, "Systems Analysis and Computer Functions," in *Institute on Automation in Large Libraries: Implications for the Administrator and the Manager, May 9-11, 1968* (Montreal: Ecole de Bibliotheconomie et Service d'education permanente, Universite de Montreal, 1968), p. 11.

[2] Louis Schultheiss, "Systems Analysis and Planning," in *Data Processing in Public and University Libraries*, John Harvey, ed. (Washington: Spartan Books, 1966), pp. 97-98.

[3] F. Bernice Field, "Anglo-American Cataloging Rules Correlated with ALA Cataloging Rules," in *New Rules for an Old Game*, pp. 137-59.

[4] *AACR*, p. 5.

[5] *Ibid.*, pp. 9-10.

[6] *Ibid.*, p. 33

[7] *Ibid.*, p. 59.

[8] *Ibid.*, p. 33.

[9] F. Bernice Field, "New Catalog Code: The General Principles and the Major Changes," *Library Resources and Technical Services*, X, (Fall 1966), 424.

CHAPTER VII

TITLE UNIT ENTRY

Conclusions

The discussions and analyses in the preceding chapters confirm the statement that "the *rules* for the choice of entry in the *Anglo-American Cataloging Rules, 1967,* based on the determination of authorship principle, fail to provide an objective means for determining the entry that will preserve the stated functions of the catalog." As a system of instructions, the rules are disorganized, complex, and ambiguous.

It has been apparent that the main author entry is a tradition much emphasized and accepted in the Western world. The reasons attached to the importance of the main entry, however, are perplexing. The present research has been concerned with the fact that the main entry principle is very much based on the determination of authorship responsibility. An attempt has been made throughout to show that neither the rules nor practice can result in objectively selected main entries. Although the rules require entering a book under the name of some person or some corporate heading, whether it is the author or not, and whether it is on the title page or not, we find that main entries are made under entries other than the author, such as titles, uniform titles or form headings. As a matter of fact, only a few rules, 28 percent, will definitely make possible the choice of an author as the main entry. These few rules deal either with works of single authorship, those where authorship responsibility has been clearly stated, or those which allow for a choice between one author and another. On the other hand, 19 percent of the rules could possibly result in the choice of an author as main entry. These rules allow for the choice between an author and another entity which is not an author, such as title, uniform title, etc. And finally, the remaining 52 percent, or the majority of the rules, cannot possibly result in the choice of an author as a main entry. All of them prescribe main entries under entities other than an author. Usually when a title is chosen as a main entry it is as a last resort because no author can be found. In some cases, however, this condition is contradicted and main title entries are made even when an author exists, such as in the case where the authors are more than three.

Above all it is clear that the determination of the main entries according to the rules is a rather complex process and one which can result in inconsistent, arbitrary, or subjective decisions. The selection of the main entry, as specified by the rules, requires a considerable amount of decision making and searching through reference sources, which is both time-consuming and costly. On the average, the selection of a main entry by a rule might require 42 steps of decisions and processes. According to the subrules this might require an average of 8 decisions and processes. Depending on the number of references given by a rule and the nature of the item being cataloged, the number of decisions required might double or triple.

Meanwhile, the decisions made, with the exception of those involving single authorship and shared authorship where responsibility of authorship is specifically indicated, are uncertain or based on personal judgment. Even in those cases where authorship is certain, it can happen that the main entry is not made under the author. An example of this is when the publication is of special kind, such as a legal or religious publication. Here the main entry preferred might be, for instance, a form heading or a uniform title.

Subjectivity in selecting main entries is illustrated by the case of a book entered under the author "first named on the title page" and by the case where a condition is given: if he is "important" or his contribution is "significant." The rules are wide open to different interpretations by different catalogers. This makes for inconsistent decisions and results in a diversity of entries for the same book which quite obviously denies the uniformity in cataloging which is a primary objective of cataloging rules. In particular, it falsifies the claim made by *AACR* and many others that the main entry is a "standard mode of identifying bibliographic entities, in all library, bibliographical, and book trade activities."[1] In works of multiple authorship where none of the authors of the publication is represented as a principal author, and works of diffused authorship, much unfairness results from the rules. While all the authors have equal share of responsibility, the rules require that one author must be selected as the main entry and given a primary role of responsibility over the other authors. It would seem that rules structured on the basis of determination of authorship responsibility to select main entries and to distinguish between main and added entries cannot be free from subjectivity. Whenever a rule uses phrases such as "if there is doubt," "if known," "if real person," the decision made according to the rule will always be based on personal judgment.

The complexity of the rules, as well as the subjectivity in selecting main entries, makes the programming of the rules for computer applications unfeasible and impractical. Much value judgment and human interference is required. Further, from the point of view of computers, the selection of main entries and even the form of heading seems unnecessary. All entries are equal as points of retrieval, and truncated entries are successfully used for obtaining the required information.

Throughout the history of cataloging, rules for the choice of entry have always been designed to provide guidance in the selection of "main" and "added" entries which would enable the user of the catalog to locate a given book whose author and/or title is known. While there is evidence in the literature, in particular in catalog-use studies, that the primary purpose of the catalog is to enable the user to locate a specific book, there is also evidence that it is a very small number of users who turn to the catalog in order to

130

locate all or any books a given author may have written. Yet the assembly of literary units is considered a fundamental function of the catalog. And the main entry under author is regarded as vital to the existence of this function.

The present study has shown, however, that the main entry's role in assembling literary units is at best only partial. Of the 129 rules in *AACR* Chapter 1, only 12 percent accomplish the assembling of literary units by means of the main entry alone. Most of these rules deal with single authorship. Moreover, 17 percent of the rules result in main entries which fail to assemble literary units. In these cases the main entries selected are under uniform title, form headings, etc. The remainder of the rules, or 70 percent, assemble literary units using a combination of main and added entries and cross references. In some of these cases one of the authors is selected as a main entry and added entries are made for the other authors. In others the main entry chosen is the title, form heading, conventional title, etc. Often this is the case even though the author's name appears on the title page of a book, which means literary units can be assembled only with the use of added entries. It has been seen also that out of the 107 rules which are intended to contribute to the assembling of literary units, 50 percent lead to incomplete literary units. This happens when added entries are not required for all the authors on the title page of a book. Thus, literary units seem to be important in some cases but not in others. Also, the main entry contributes to the assembling of literary units in some cases but not in others.

Actually, it would seem that the assembling of literary units is not so much a question of main and added entries; rather, it is a question of form of heading inasmuch as whatever entry is provided—"main" or "added"—no literary units can be assembled without the right form of heading and/or necessary cross references. Assembling literary units for an author requires, first, the making of an entry for him if he is represented on the title page of a book, and second, either entering all his works under one form of his name, if he has more than one, and making *see* references from all the other forms, or entering his works under the various forms of his name and connecting these by *see also* references. In other words, the assembly of literary units is primarily a function of the form of heading and cross references, and not so much a function of main and/or added entries.

It has been advanced that the main entry serves another purpose with regard to assembling literary units. It is held that the main entry is necessary also for assembling literary units under added entries and subject headings. This, however, is equally questionable. For instance, many books do not have a main author entry and many other books have more than one author. In both cases the assembly of literary units under a subject heading will be partial. Usually added entries are not made under subject headings and, further, many books are not even assigned subject headings. As a consequence, not all of an author's books will be listed under a subject heading; and even if all of an author's books are assigned subject headings, there is no guarantee that all of them will be under the same subject heading or the same subdivision of one subject heading. Similarly, in many cases added entries are not made for all of the authors on the title page of a book. Thus, the main entry will assemble literary units under some added entries and not under the others. Again, its role is partial.

Actually, assembling literary units under added entries or subject headings seems to be unimportant from the point of view of practice. Many libraries do not subarrange their added entries or subject headings by main entry. Instead they subarrange them by title. Even ALA filing rules recommend this practice for added entries.

It is clear that the *AACR* devotes a great many rules and a great deal of space to the choice of main entries and to the distinction between main and added entries. The functions of main and added entries are not different, inasmuch as both are used in identifying a given known book in the catalog and in assembling literary units. Would not much energy and time be saved if the distinction were abandoned? Given these considerations, is not the *title unit entry* a much more objective and simpler approach to the cataloging of library materials and to the fulfilling of the objectives of the catalog? Insofar as the title unit entry requires no rules for the choice of entry, it represents a mechanical approach to main entry cataloging. It is true that rules for description, added entries and form of headings are required, but these are also required for the main entry practice now in use.

Recommendations

In light of the above considerations the first and most important recommendation to be made is that the main entry principle be abandoned from our cataloging theory and practice and be replaced by the title unit entry. Consequently the following changes in *AACR* are proposed:

1. The first thirty-two rules of Chapter 1 in *AACR* entitled "Entry" should be deleted from the Code.
2. Since the Standard for Bibliographic Description (ISBD) enumerates requirements for the title unit entry, it should be incorporated as Chapter 1 of the Code. A provision, however, must be made in ISBD to the effect that the author statement must always be added after the title of the book.
3. To provide author and other entries necessary for the retrieval of an item, a rule for added entries should be included in the first chapter for description. A revised version of Rule 33 might read as follows:
   Rule #
   Preliminary note: Entries are important for retrieval purposes and for providing direct access to bibliographical items that are represented in the catalog. The following rules state the general principles for making entries. If it is desired to have the catalog display fully the significant bibliographic activities of each person or corporate body, insofar as these are represented by the works that have been cataloged, it will be necessary to go beyond these rules. The extent to which a library may desire to make analytical entries to display parts of the bibliographic units that have been cataloged is a matter of local library policy, being related to the extent of the

collection, the needs of the clientele, and the special considerations involved in each instance.

A. General Rule

Make an entry under any person or corporate body[2] associated[3] with the publication, following the guidelines of Rules B-E.

B. Collaborator

Make an entry for each of as many as three collaborating authors whether there are three or more on the title page. Make an entry for each of three collaborating personal authors if there is a corporate body involved.[4]

FIGURE 12

Title page: Pain and Emotion// by Roger Trigg.// Oxford Press. Oxford// 1970.

Title Unit Entry

```
        Pain and emotion, by Roger Trigg.
    Oxford, Clarendon P., 1970.
        viii, 187p.  22cm.  index.

    Bibliography:  p.  [180]-183.


        1. Pain - Psychological aspects.  2.
    Emotion.  I. Trigg, Roger.

    BF515.T75
```

FIGURE 13

Title page: The Political Diaries of C.P. Scott 1911-1928.∥ Edited with an introduction and commentary by Trevor Wilson.∥ Cornell University Press, Ithaca, New York.∥ **Date on verso of title page**: 1970

Title Unit Entry

```
      The Political diaries of C.P. Scott,
1911-1928.    Edited with an introd. and
commentary by Trevor Wilson.    Ithaca, N.Y.,
Cornell University Press [1970]
      509p.  ports,  24cm.

  Includes bibliographical references.
  1. Gt. Brit. - Politics and government -
1910-1936.  I. Scott, Charles Prestwich,
1846-1932.  II. Wilson, Trevor, 1928-      ed.


DA576.S35  1970
```

FIGURE 14

Title page: Immunology∥ by Sverre Dick Henriksen, M.D.∥ Universitetsforlaget 1970.∥ Oslo-Bergen-Tromso∥ **On verso of title page**: Translated by Gro Blystad.

Title Unit Entry

```
      Immunology, by Sverre Dick Henriksen.
[Translated by Gro Blystad]    Oslo, Univer-
sitetsforlaget; Baltimore, Williams and
Wilkins Co. [1970]
      182p.  illus.  23cm.

  Bibliography:  p.174-177.

  1. Immunology.  I. Henriksen, Sverre
Dick, 1906-      II. Blystad, Gro., tr.

QR180.H4
```

FIGURE 15

Title page: The Brownings: Letters and Poetry.// Selected and with an introduction by Christopher Ricks.// Illustrations by Bernett I. Plotkin.// **Date from verso of title page**: 1970

Title Unit Entry

```
     The Brownings:  letters and poetry.
Selected and with an introd. by Christopher
Ricks.  Illus. by Barnett I. Plotkin.
Garden City, N.Y., Doubleday [1970]
     xi, 726p.  2 ports.  22cm.


     I. Ricks, Christopher B., comp.  II.
Browning, Robert, 1812-1889.  III. Browning,
Elizabeth (Barrett) 1806-1861. 1v.  Plotkin,
Barnett I., illus.
PR4203.R5 1970b
```

FIGURE 16

Title page: College Students on Chronic Wards// by Karl E. Scheibe, James A. Kulik, Paul D. Hersch, and Sherry LaMacchia.// Behavioral Publications,// New York.// **From other parts of the book**: c 1969; Community Mental Health Journal. Monograph series no. 5.

Title Unit Entry

```
     College students on chronic wards, by
Karl E. Scheibe, James A. Kulik, Paul D.
Hersch, et. al.  New York, Behavioral
Publications [c1969]
     33p.  23cm.  (Community mental health
journal.  Monograph series, no.5)
     Bibliography:  p.33.
     1. Volunteer workers in mental health.
2. Psychiatric hospitals - Sociological
aspects.  I. Scheibe, Karl E.  II. Kulik,
James A.  III. Hersch, Paul D.  IV. Series.

RC439.C66
```

FIGURE 17

Title page: Ranking & Spicer's Company Law.// Eleventh edition// by R.E.G. Perrins and A. Jeffreys.// H.F.L. (Publishers) Ltd.// London// **Date from verso of title page**: 1970

Title Unit Entry

```
        Ranking & Spicer's company law.   11th ed.
   by R.E.G. Perrins and A. Jeffreys.    London,
   H.F.L. Publishers [1970]
        xlvii, 427p  23cm.


        1. Corporation law - Gt. Brit.  I. Rank-
   ing, Devey Fearon de l'Hoste, 1847 or 8-1931.
   II. Spicer, Ernest Evan. III. Perrins, R.E.G.
   IV. Jeffreys, A.
```

FIGURE 18

Title page: Essays in Shakesperean criticism// edited by James L. Calderwood, Harold E. Toliver.// Prentice Hall, Inc.// Englewood Cliffs, New Jersey// **Date from verso of title page**: 1970

Title Unit Entry

```
        Essays in Shakespearean criticism.
   Edited by James L. Calderwood [and]
   Harold E. Toliver.    Englewood Cliffs, N.J.,
   Prentice-Hall [1970]
        xiv, 590p.  23cm.

        Includes bibliographical references.

        1. Shakespeare, William, 1564-1616 -
   Criticism and interpretation.  I. Calder-
   wood, James L., comp. II. Toliver, Harold
   E., comp.
   PR2890.C33
```

FIGURE 19

Title page: Communicating by Satellite.// An International Discussion.// Report of an International conference sponsored by the Carnegie Endowment for International Peace and the Twentieth Century Fund// by Gordon L. Weil.// Carnegie Endowment for International Peace / New York// Twentieth Century Fund/ New York// 1969

Title Unit Entry

```
        Communicating by satellite:  an inter-
    national discussion [edited] by Gordon L.
    Weil.   New York, Carnegie Endowment for
    International Peace, 1969.
        vii, 30p.  23cm.
    Report of an international conference
    sponsored by the Carnegie Endowment for
    International Peace and the Twentieth
    Century Fund; held at Talloires, France,
    Sept.21-25, 1969.
        1. Artificial satellites in telecommuni-
    cation.  I. Weil, Gordon Lee, ed.
    II. Carnegie Endowment for International
    Peace.  III. Twentieth Century Fund.
    HE9719.C6
```

FIGURE 20

Title page: Knowledge and Necessity.// Royal Institute of Philosophy Lectures Volume three. 1968-1969// Macmillan// St. Martin's Press// **Date from verso of title page**: 1970

Title Unit Entry

```
        Knowledge and necessity.   [London]
    Macmillan; [New York] St. Martin's Press
    [1970]
        xxi, 284p  23cm.  (Royal Institute of
    Philosophy lectures, v.3, 1968-1969)
        Includes bibliographical references.

        1. Knowledge, Theory of - Addresses,
    essays, lectures.  I. Royal Institute of
    Philosophy.  II. Series.

    BD161.R73 1970
```

137

FIGURE 21

Title page: Exploding Humanity the crisis of numbers.// Edited by Henry Regier and J. Bruce Falls.// Anansi Toronto 1969// **From other parts of the book**: The proceedings of the fourth International Teach-in University of Toronto—1968, Sponsored by the International Forum Foundation

Title Unit Entry

```
       Exploding humanity; the crisis of numbers.
   Edited by Henry Regier and J. Bruce Falls.
   Toronto, Anansi, 1969.
       188p.  23cm.
   "The proceedings of the fourth Interna-
   tional Teach-in, University of Toronto--
   1968," sponsored by the International Forum
   Foundation.
       Includes bibliographies.
```

```
        Exploding humanity.   (Card 2)


       1. Population - Congresses.  2. Birth
   control - Congresses.  I. Toronto Inter-
   national Teach-in, 4th, 1968.  II. Regier,
   Henry A., 1930-       ed.  III. Falls, James
   Bruce, 1923-       ed.  IV. Toronto.  Univer-
   sity.  V. International Forum Foundation.
   HB849.T67 1968
```

C. Persons Identified Cryptically

When added entries are required for persons who can be identified only by cryptic indications found in the publication being cataloged, make them in the manner indicated below.

1) Initials and abbreviations of name. If the only clue to a person's name is the appearance in the publication of initials or abbreviations of the name, make two entries: one in direct

order, and one transposed to bring the supposed initial or abbreviation of his surname into first position. Follow the provisions of Chapter 2 for all questions of form. Include any typographical devices that follow an initial. When it is clear that the initials stand for the name of a corporate body, however, make a single added entry in direct order.

On title page:	von M.B.
Entries:	M.B.
	B., M.

On title page:	par mr. l'abbé de B. . .
Entry:	B. . ., abbé de

On title page:	By Th. B., B.D.
Entries:	Th. B., B.D.
	B., Th., B.D.

Signed:	E. B-s
Entries:	E. B-s
	B-s, E.

On title page:	by A. De O.
Entries:	A. De O.
	De O., A.

2) Phrases. Make an entry under a concise phrase that characterizes the person and provides the only clue to his identity.

On title page:	by a physician
Entry:	a physician

On title page:	by an American
Entry:	An American

3) "Author of" statement. When the author is indicated only as the author of another work, transpose the statement to bring the title into first position.

On title page:	by the author of Early Impressions
Entry:	Early Impressions, Author of

D. Analytical Entries

When warranted by local circumstances, make analytical author, title or author-title entries, beyond those specified in the rules, to reveal the contents of a publication.

E. Series

Make an entry under the series for each separately cataloged work (adding after the title the numerical designation of the work as part of the series if it is numbered). Entries are only rarely made, however, if all the volumes in the series are by the same person. Entries are not generally made for:

1) series with titles that include the name of a trade publisher

139

(e.g., Bibliotèque autodidactique Quillet) or that do not have a subject limitation and which may have only format in common (e.g., Mentor executive library, published by New American Library, or Coleccion azul);

2) series with numbering that suggests that the parts have been numbered primarily for stock control (e.g., many paperback series) or to benefit from lower mailing rates (e.g., some university bulletins that embrace most of the institution's publications).

F. Titles

1) Make a title entry for every title-page title of a book.[5]

2) Make a title entry for titles other than the main title (cover title, partial title, binders title) when these differ from the title-page title, etc.

3) Make an added entry for uniform titles.

FIGURE 22

Title page: Tales from the Arabian Nights.// Illustrated by Brian Wildsmith.// H.Z. Walck New York 1962// **From other parts of the book**: Adapted from Lane's translation.

Title Unit Entry

```
    Tales from the Arabian nights.  Illus-
trated by Brian Wildsmith.   New York,
H.Z. Walck, 1962.
    281 p. col. illus. 22 cm.

    "Adapted from Edward William Lane's
translation."


    I. Title: Arabian Nights.   II. Wildsmith,
Brian, Illus.
    PJ7715.L3
```

4) In the case where the uniform title is of the type made up by the cataloger, such as Works, Selected Works, etc., make an author-title entry.

It is obvious that the system of rules required for making title unit entries is simpler than that required for making main entries. It is simpler because it reduces the amount of decision making as well as the kind of decision making. All books are described in the same manner, with the title standing as the first element of the description. The identification of the book and the assembling of literary units for authors can then be provided through entries such as entries for author(s), contributor(s), translator(s), editor(s), etc., and the title.

The adoption of the title unit entry would have considerable advantages:

1. It would eliminate the need for personal judgments required by the present rules. Thus, it would eliminate the discrepancies and inconsistencies which now characterize catalog entries. In so doing, it would bring uniformity and standardization to cataloging practice. Catalogers in any library would be able to enter the same book under the same heading. Not only would this facilitate local as well as international cooperation and transfer of bibliographical information between libraries, it would also eliminate costly duplication of effort.

2. Where there is multiple diffused authorship, the title unit entry concept considers all authors as equal and all are given entries on the same level. No one author is given recognition or primary responsibility by presenting him in a preeminent position. In this sense it would seem that the title unit entry recognition of authorship is much fairer than the main entry concept.

3. Because of the simplicity of the title unit entry, the descriptive cataloging process would be transformed into a more or less mechanical operation, one that could be performed by non-professional staff. This would result in major savings for libraries now faced with ever-increasing processing costs.

4. Finally, use of the title unit entry would reduce the time and effort spent on the selection of the so-called "main entry," which, as we have seen, serves no important purpose in the catalog. This would relieve the staff to perform other more important duties; the processing and the availability of library materials to the user would be speeded up; costs of processing would be reduced.

Two problems still have not been touched upon in this discussion of title unit *versus* main entry. First is the problem of assigning book numbers. The following two rules give some guidance in the use of book numbers with Dewey Decimal Classification and with the Library of Congress Classification when appropriate:

1. General rule: Assign the book number according to the first author entry if there is any, otherwise according to the title.

2. In the case of form headings and conventional titles, the book number is assigned according to the title page title of the book in hand.[6]

The second problem has to do with the administrative implications of adopting the title unit entry. These questions might be asked: How will the adoption of the title unit entry affect present catalogs constructed according to the main entry? Would recataloging of older publications be necessary? Would the changeover increase the expenses of processing? The answers to all these questions is "no." The title unit entry will not affect the structure of the catalog in any way. We presently make title main entries for many books. All that is involved is that instead of adopting such entries for some books and not others, we adopt them for all books. Moreover, no recataloging of older materials would be required. The integration of the new and the old is simply a continuance of the present integration of title main entries and author main entries. Thus, no additional costs would be involved. Rather, as we mentioned earlier, many savings could be realized in several areas of library technical operations.

It has been shown that searching by titles is a more reliable approach than searching by main entry. Inherent in titles are mnemonic features which allow them, as compared with authors, to be more accurately remembered by the user. Titles, more than authors, contribute to the matching and retrieval of bibliographic information. Titles also represent a more straightforward approach, since each book has its own unique title. Lubetzky's assumption that title added entries for non-distinctive titles and titles which parallel subject headings confuse the user and substantially increase the size of the catalog, is not really substantiated. Use studies discussed in this investigation indicate that any confusion which exists may very well be due to the inconsistent and partial coverage of titles in the catalog. As to the use of the catalog by the library staff, the title approach is favored and advocated for searching as it is more reliable and less costly. With respect to increasing the size of the catalog, it was found in the title catalog reconstruction project at the University of Wisconsin—Milwaukee that the number of titles that had been omitted was not large. It might generally be that completing a catalog would contribute only a little to the bulk of the catalog.

The above arguments for the importance of the title entry as a finding approach suggest two further recommendations. The first is that title entries should be made for each book title. This would insure title coverage in the catalog, make the catalog a more reliable tool and eliminate users' confusion. Following this recommendation would result in advantages relating to library operations. Making title entries would eliminate: 1) the unnecessary time spent by the staff on the complex process of identifying main entries for acquisitions and cataloging purposes, which would reduce costs of processing and increase the efficiency of the staff; 2) duplication in acquisitions of library materials, thereby providing another saving; 3) the cataloger's personal judgment as to whether titles should be given added entries on the basis of distinctiveness or the existence of parallel subject headings; and 4) time spent on catalog maintenance, especially time spent adding titles which for some reason have been omitted. One wonders how much libraries have really saved by not making title entries for all books in the first place.

The second recommendation is that rather than author catalogs, title catalogs with author indexes should be adopted. Title arrangement can insure the uniformity and standardization of bibliographical tools, especially single entry tools, and thus make the use of these tools easier and faster. Also, cooperation in cataloging would be facilitated.

A problem which was discussed and which is related to cataloging rules in general is the diversity and variation in title pages. Title pages of books vary considerably in completeness and structure. This diversity has the effect of complicating the rules, that is, the rules must be expanded to deal with special cases. What this suggests is the need for standardization of the title pages of books. Also, standardization is very much called for, considering that mechanized descriptive cataloging by means of optical scanning techniques is expected in the near future. Although standardization of title pages is necessary, it is perhaps impractical. Book production is an art which should be preserved. Book collectors, libraries, printers and publishers all alike probably wish to maintain their individuality.

A solution to this problem might be that instead of standardizing the original title page of every book, an extra standardized title page could be inserted in the book to meet the needs of automated operations. This page would be standardized not only in organization and structure but also, for instance, with respect to type font to meet the requirements of optical scanning.

Although this study has been limited to rules governing monographic publications, the concept of the title unit entry is applicable to and recommended for all other types of library materials. In the area of non-book materials the practice of title unit entry has been recommended by several specialists in the field.[7] Thus, the rules governing the choice of entry for non-book materials might well be deleted along the same lines recommended for rules governing monographic publication.

Areas for Further Study

The methodology used in the present study appears to have worked well in determining whether or not the practice of main entry is a reasonable means for fulfilling the objectives of the catalog and whether or not the rules governing its choice lead to objective decisions. System analysis techniques in particular, flowcharting—seem to be especially suitable for studying the logical organization and efficiency of systems of instructions or procedures. Moreover, studies applying the same methodology to rules other than main entry rules in *AACR*, such as the rules for the form of heading and description, might be equally rewarding.

This study has shown the need for information on situational factors relating to the use of the main entry. Fundamental data on the time and money spent on the determination of the main entries is very much needed. Also, similar data on the time and money spent searching by library staff when the main entry approach is used would be of great value. Further, a study of the amount of the duplication in acquisitions of library materials which results because of a reliance on the main entry in the searching and organization of library files might be an interesting area of exploration. Ideally, these studies should be done on a comparative basis.

FOOTNOTES

[1] *AACR*, p. 2.

[2] If the responsibility of the content of the work appears to extend beyond that of issuing body or financial underwriter.

[3] Include author, writer, editor, compiler, translator, illustrator, etc. No discrimination should be made on the basis of importance or significance. All those associated with the work, with its intellectual content or in some other way, should be identified by entries.

[4] Although the decision based on the number three is as arbitrary as that made by *AACR*, this rule has two advantages: a) it makes the rule of three consistent with every book cataloged; b) it provides more access points than one author. For example, the chances of finding a book with ten authors will be three out of ten instead of one out of ten.

[5] Libraries wishing exceptions can follow those provided by *AACR*.

[6] *Ibid.*

[7] This rule would eliminate crowding the shelf list under a given popular letter.

[8] Jay E. Daily, "The Selection, Processing, and Storage of Nonprint Materials: A Critique of the Anglo-American Cataloging Rules as They Relate to Newer Media," *Library Trends*, XVI (October 1967), 283-89; Lewis, *op. cit.*; Hicks and Tillin, *op. cit.*; Walter W. Ristow, "The Emergence of Maps in Libraries," *Special Libraries*, LVIII (July 1967), 400-19.

SELECTED BIBLIOGRAPHY

"AA Cataloging Code," by Andrew D. Osborn. Review of *Anglo-American Cataloging Rules*, North American text. *Library Journal*, XCIII (October 1, 1968), 3523-25.

A.L.A. Cataloging Rules: Author and Title Entries. Prepared by the Catalog Code Revision Committee of the American Library Association, with the collaboration of the Committee of the (British) Library Association. Preliminary American 2d ed. Chicago: American Library Association, 1941.

ALA Cataloging Rules for Author and Title Entries. Prepared by Division of Cataloging and Classification, American Library Association. Edited by Clara Beetle. 2d ed. Chicago: American Library Association, 1949.

ALA Rules for Filing Catalog Cards. Prepared by the American Library Association Editorial Committee's Subcommittee on the ALA Rules for Filing Catalog Cards. Edited by Pauline A. Seely. 2d ed. Chicago: American Library Association, 1968.

"ALA to AA, an Obstacle Race," by Pauline A. Seely. *Library Resources and Technical Services*, XIII (Winter 1969), 7-25.

"Access and Recognition: From Users' Data to Catalogue Entries," by Renata Tagliacozzo. *Journal of Documentation*, XXVI (September 1970), 230-49.

"Administrative Implications of the New Rules," by J. A. Rosenthal. *Library Resources and Technical Services*, X (Fall 1966), 437-44.

"Alternative Headings," by A. E. Jeffreys. *Catalogue and Index*, No. 8 (October 1967), 4-5.

American National Standard for Title Leaves of a Book. New York: American National Standards Institute, 1971.

"An Argument Against the Use of Conventional Headings in the Cataloging of Primary Legal Sources," by D. Dean Willard. *Library Resources and Technical Services*, XIII (Summer 1969), 198-202.

"An Investigation of Main Entry Approach for Search of Request Cards," by Sybil S. Donaldson. Unpublished paper presented to 350 Seminar in Technical Services, University of Pittsburgh Graduate School of Library and Information Sciences, 1969. (Typewritten.)

Anglo-American Cataloging Rules. Prepared by the American Library Association, the Library of Congress, the Library Association, and the Canadian Library Association. North American text. Chicago: American Library Association, 1967.

145

"Anglo-American Cataloging Rules; Headings for Corporate Bodies," by F. Hinton. *Library Resources and Technical Services*, XIII (Winter 1969), 47-61.

"Anglo-American Cataloging Rules 1967," by J. C. Downing. *Library World*, LXX (February 1969), 199-204.

"The Anglo-American Cataloging Rules, 1967," by James A. Tait. *Library Review*, XXI (Summer 1967), 69-74.

"Anglo-American Cataloging Rules: Selection and Form of Entry," by Carolyn A. Small. *Library Resources and Technical Services*, XIII (Winter 1969), 26-31.

"Author Bibliographies," by A. E. Day. *Library Review*, XXI (Summer 1967), 81-83.

"Author versus Title: A Comparative Survey of the Accuracy of the Information which the User Brings to the Library Catalogue," by F. H. Ayers. *Journal of Documentation*, XXIV (December 1968), 266-72.

Authors and Titles; an Analytical Study of the Author Concept in Codes of Cataloging Rules in the English Language, from that of the British Museum in 1841, to the Anglo-American Cataloging Rules, 1967, by James A. Tait. Hamden, Conn.: Archon Books, 1969; London: Clive Bingley, Ltd., 1969.

The Backs of Books and Other Essays in Librarianship, by William Warner Bishop. Baltimore: Williams and Wilkins, 1926.

Bibliographic Automation of Large Library Operations Using a Time-sharing System: Phase I, Final Report, by A. H. Epstein, *et al.* Stanford University Libraries, 1971.

"Bibliographic Description, Arrangement and Retrieval," by B. C. Vickery. *Journal of Documentation*, XXIV (March 1968), 1-15.

"Binder's Title," by Jay E. Daily. *Encyclopedia of Library and Information Science*. Vol. II. New York: Marcel Dekker, 1969.

"The Bitter End," by Ashby J. Fristoe. *Library Resources and Technical Services*, X (Winter 1966), 91-95.

"A Book Catalog at Stanford," by Richard D. Johnson. *Journal of Library Automation*, I (March 1968), 13-50.

"Book Catalogs," by Ralph H. Parker. *Library Resources and Technical Services*, VIII (Fall 1964), 344-48.

The Brasenose Conference on the Automation of Libraries; Proceedings of the Anglo-American Conference on the Mechanization of Library Services Held at Oxford Under the Chairmanship of Sir Frank Francis and Sponsored by the Old Dominion Foundation of New York, 30 June–3 July 1966. Edited by John Harrison and Peter Laslett. London: Mansell, 1967.

"Bridging the Gap Between Cataloging and Information Retrieval," by Doralyn J. Hickey. *Library Resources and Technical Services*, XI (Summer 1967), 173-83.

"A Brief History of Cataloging Codes in the United States, 1852-1949," by Vivian Davidson Palmer. Unpublished Master's thesis, University of Chicago Graduate Library School, 1963.

"Card Catalog Arrangement," by George Scheerer. *Library Resources and Technical Services*, XIII (Winter 1969), 7-25.

The Catalog and Cataloging, selected by Arthur Roy Rowland. Hamden, Conn.: Shoe String Press, 1969.

Catalog Card Reproduction Project, by Joseph R. Edelen. Vermillion, S.D.: I.D. Weeks Library, University of South Dakota, 1971.

Catalog Rules: Author and Title Entries. Compiled by committees of the American Library Association and the (British) Library Association. American ed. Chicago: ALA, Publishing Board, 1908.

Catalog Use Study, by Sidney L. Jackson. Edited by Vaclav Mostecky. Chicago: American Library Association, 1958.

"Cataloging and CCS: 1957-1966," by Paul S. Dunkin. *Library Resources and Technical Services*, XI (Summer 1967), 267-88.

Cataloging and Classification, an Introductory Manual, by Thelma Eaton. 4th ed. Ann Arbor, Mich.: Edwards Brothers, Inc., 1967.

"Cataloging and Classification of Arabic Books, Some Basic Considerations," by Mahmoud el-Sheniti. *UNESCO Bulletin for Libraries*, XIV (May-June, 1960), 104-106.

Cataloging Cost Study in Five Small Public Libraries, by Patricia Ann Sacks. Rochester, N.Y.: University of Rochester Press for the Association of College and Research Libraries, 1967.

Cataloging for Library Technical Assistants, by Jay E. Daily and Mildred Myers, with the assistance of George M. Sinkankas. Washington, D.C.: Communication Service Corporation, 1969.

"The Cataloging of Publications of Corporate Authors," by Mortimer Taube. *Library Quarterly*, XX (January 1950), 1-20.

"The Cataloging of Publications of Corporate Authors: A Rejoiner," by Seymour Lubetzky. *Library Quarterly*, XXI (January 1951), 1-12.

Cataloging Policy Objectives and the Computer: a Paper Presented to the Catalogue Working Party of the Libraries and Computers Group on the 7th of September, 1966, by Alferd David Burnett. Durham, Eng.: A.D. Burnett, 1966.

"Cataloging Principles. Five Years after the Paris Conference," by Arthur Hugh Chaplin. *UNESCO Bulletin for Libraries*, XXI (May-June 1967), 140-45, 149.

"Cataloging Rules." *Library Resources and Technical Services*, VIII (Summer 1964), 299-301.

Cataloging Rules and Principles; a Critique of the ALA Rules for Entry and a Proposed Design for Their Revision, by Seymour Lubetzky. Washington, D.C.: Processing Department, Library of Congress, 1953.

Cataloging Service. Bulletin, No. 1– ; June 1945– . Washington, D.C.: Library of Congress, Descriptive Cataloging Division.

"Cataloging: Some New Approaches; What Price the Main Entry?" by Henry A. Sharp. *Library World*, LVII (January 1956), 113-16.

Cataloging Theory and Practice, by C. G. Viswanathan, 3d ed. London: Asia Publishing, 1966.

Cataloging U.S.A., by Paul S. Dunkin. Chicago: American Library Association, 1969.

"Catalogs and Cataloging," by Eugene R. Hanson and Jay E. Daily. *Encyclopedia of Library and Information Science*. Vol. IV. New York: Marcel Dekker, 1970.

"Catalogs, Codes and Bibliographic Control," by Wilma Radford. *College and Research Libraries*, X (October 1949), 395-400, 428.

Cataloguing and Classification in British University Libraries: A Survey of Practices and Procedures, by Joan Friedman and Alan Jeffreys. Sheffield: Sheffield University Postgraduate School of Librarianship, 1967.

"Cataloguing and Classification in British University Libraries: A Survey of Practices and Procedures," by Joan Friedman and Alan Jeffreys. *Journal of Documentation*, XXIII (September 1967), 224-46.

"Cataloguing Comparison in an International Setting," by E. Murray. *Australian Library Journal*, XII (September 1963), 147-53.

Cataloguing Rules: A Simplified Version of Library Association and American Library Association Cataloguing Rules: Author and Title Entries for the Use of School Librarians, compiled by W. L. Saunders and Norman Furlong. 3d ed. London: School Library Association, 1966.

"The Choice of Entry of Books; a Comparative Study of Principles and Rules Which Govern It, with Special Attention to Some Problems Concerning the Entry of Arabic Books," by Muhammed el-Mahdi. Unpublished Master's thesis, Cairo University, Faculty of Arts, 1961.

The Classification of Maps and Atlases, by Samuel W. Boggs and Dorothy C. Lewis. New York: Special Libraries Association, 1945.

The Code and the Cataloguer, Proceedings of the Colloquium on the Anglo-American Cataloguing Rules Held at the School of Library Science, University of Toronto on March 31 and April 1, 1967. Edited by Katharine H. Packer, Delores Phillips, and Katharine L. Ball. Toronto: University of Toronto Press, 1969.

Code of Cataloging Rules: Author and Title Entry; an Unfinished Draft for a New Edition of Cataloging Rules Prepared for the Catalog Code Revision Committee, by Seymour Lubetzky. With an Explanatory Commentary by Paul Dunkin. Chicago: American Library Association, 1960.

A Comparative Study of Cataloging Rules Based on the Anglo-American Code of 1908, by J.C.M. Hanson. Chicago: University of Chicago Press, 1939.

"Computer-produced Book Catalogs: Entry Form and Content," by Edward A. Weinstein. *Library Resources and Technical Services*, XI (Summer 1967), 185-91.

Computer Programming Fundamentals, by Herbert D. Leeds and Gerald M. Weinberg. New York: Mc-Graw Hill, 1961.

Computerized Library Catalogs; Their Growth, Cost, and Utility, by J. L. Dolby, V. J. Forsyth and H. L. Resinkoff. Cambridge, Mass.: M.I.T. Press, 1969.

Computerizing the Card Catalog in the University Library; a Survey of User Requirements, by Richard P. Palmer. Littleton, Colo.: Libraries Unlimited, Inc., 1972.

"Concept of an On-line Computerized Library Catalog," by Frederick G. Kilgour. *Journal of Library Automation*, III (March 1970), 1-11.

Conversion of Retrospective Catalog Records to Machine-readable Form; a Study of the Feasibility of a National Bibliographic Service. Prepared by the RECON Working Task Force, Henriette D. Avram, William R. Nugent, Josephine S. Pulsifer and others. Edited by John C. Rather. Washington, D.C.: Library of Congress, 1969.

"Corporate Authorship and Cultural Evolution," by R. Taylor. *Library Resources and Technical Services*, X (Fall 1966), 451-54.

"Corporate Authorship versus Title Entry," by J.C.M. Hanson. *Library Quarterly*, V (October 1935), 457-66.

"Crisis in Cataloging," by Andrew D. Osborn. *Library Quarterly*, XI (October 1941), 393-411.

Cutting Costs in Acquisitions and Cataloging; Proceedings, AALL Institute for Law Librarians June 15-19, 1969, Grossing, New York. Directed by Marian G. Gallagher. South Hackensack, N.J.: F. B. Rothman for American Association of Law Libraries, 1960.

"Danger—Code Erosion! An Anglo-American Exchange of Notes." *Catalogue and Index*, No. 14 (April 1969), 1.

Data Processing in Public and University Libraries. Edited by John Harvey. Washington, D.C.: Spartan Books, 1966.

Descriptive Cataloging, by Andrew D. Osborn. Preliminary ed. Pittsburgh: University of Pittsburgh Graduate Library School, 1963.

Developing Multi-Media Libraries, by Warren B. Hicks and Alma M. Tillin. New York: R.R. Bowker, 1970.

"The Development of Authorship Entry and the Formulation of Authorship Rules as Found in the Anglo-American Code," by Julia Pettee. *Library Quarterly*, VI (July 1936), 270-90.

"The Development of the Catalog and Cataloging Codes," by Ruth French Strout. *Library Quarterly*, XXVI (October 1956), 254-75.

"Effective Main Entries: A Comparison of the ALA Cataloging Code with Seymour Lubetzky's Draft Revision in Relation to Bibliographic Citations," by Elizabeth Lamb Tate. Unpublished Ph.D. dissertation, University of Chicago Graduate Library School, 1965.

"The Emergence of Maps in Libraries," by Walter W. Ristow. *Special Libraries*, LVIII (July 1967), 400-19.

"The End of Superimposition?" by S. R. Ranganathan. *Catalogue and Index*, No. 18 (April 1970), 13.

Entries of Arabic Authors, First List up to 1215 H/1800 A.D., by Mahmoud el-Sheniti. Cairo: Egyptian Association of Archives and Libraries, 1961.

"Filing Rules for a Three-dimensional Catalog," by John Dulka and Joseph Z. Nitecki. *Library Resources and Technical Services*, XIV (Fall 1970), 485-96.

149

"A Filing System for the Machine Age," by Joseph T. Popecki. *Library Resources and Technical Services*, IX (Summer 1965), 333.

"Four-way Catalog," by Hugh E. Behymer. *Library Journal*, XCIII (March 15, 1968), 1083.

"Future Implications of Title IIC, Higher Education Act of 1965," by James E. Skipper. *Library Resources and Technical Services*, XI (Winter 1967), 46-49.

"General Philosophy and Structure of the Code," by Wyllis E. Wright. Institute on Cataloging Code Revision, Stanford University, July 9–12, 1958. *Working Papers*. Sponsored by the Cataloging and Classification Section of the Resources and Technical Services Division, American Library Association and the Stanford University Libraries. Stanford, Calif., 1958.

General Systems Theory and Psychiatry. Edited by William Gray, Frederick J. Duhl, and Nicholas D. Rizzo. Boston: Little, Brown and Company, 1969.

Headings and Canons: Comparative Study of Five Catalogue Codes, by S. R. Ranganathan. Madras: S. Viswanathan, 1955; London: G. Blunt and Sons, 1955.

"IFLA International Meeting of Cataloguing Experts, Copenhagen, 1969," by Arthur Hugh Chaplin. *Library Resources and Technical Services*, XIV (Spring 1970), 292-96.

The Identification of Data Elements in Bibliographic Records; Final Report for the Special Project on Data Elements for the Subcommittee on Machine Input Records (SC-2) of the Sectional Committee on Library Work and Documentation (Z-39) of the United States of America Standards Institute, by Ann T. Curan and Henriette D. Avram. Needham, Mass.: 1967.

"In Praise of Error; with some Animadversions on the Cost of Descriptive Cataloging," by Daniel Gore. *Library Journal*, XC (February 1, 1965), 582-85.

"The Information about Books Known by Users of the Catalog Who are Looking for a Particular Work," by Mary Blackburn. Unpublished M.A. thesis, University of Chicago Graduate Library School, 1968.

"Institute on Catalog Code Revision: A Composite Report." *Library Resources and Technical Services*, III (Spring 1959), 123-40.

International Conference on Cataloguing Principles, Paris, October 8–18th, 1961, Report. London: Organizing Committee of the International Conference on Cataloging Principles, National Central Library, 1963.

"The International Meeting of Cataloguing Experts, a Report from Copenhagen," by Michael Gorman. *Catalogue and Index*, No. 16 (October 1969), 12.

International Standard Bibliographic Description (for Single Volume and Multi-volume Monographic Publications). Recommended by the Working Group on the International Standard Bibliographic Description set up at the International Meeting of Cataloguing Experts, Copenhagen, 1969. London: IFLA Committee on Cataloguing, 1971.

"International Standard Bibliographic Description." *Cataloging Information Bulletin*, No. 104 (May 1972), 8-9.

Introduction to Cataloging, by John J. Boll. Vol. I. New York: McGraw-Hill, 1970.

Introduction to Cataloging, by John J. Boll, Peggy O'N. Parry, and Richard D. Walker. Vol. II. Preliminary ed. Madison, Wis.: Library School, University of Wisconsin, 1966.

Introduction to Cataloging and Classification, by Bohdan S. Wynar. 4th rev. ed. Littleton, Colo.: Libraries Unlimited, Inc., 1972.

Introduction to Cataloging and the Classification of Books, by Margaret Mann. 2d ed. Chicago: American Library Association, 1943.

"Italian Cataloging Rules," by Liana van der Bellen. *Library Resources and Technical Services*, X (Fall 1966), 499-504.

Library Catalogs: Changing Dimensions; The Twenty-Eighth Annual Conference of the Graduate Library School August 5-7, 1963. Edited by Ruth French Strout. Chicago: University of Chicago Press, 1964.

Library Catalogs: Their Preservation and Maintenance by Photographic and Automatic Techniques; a Study. Edited by James W. Henderson and Joseph A. Rosenthal. Cambridge, Mass.: M.I.T. Press for the New York Public Library, Astor, Lenox, and Tilden Foundations, 1968.

"Library Development in the Arab World," by F. L. Kent and F. Abu Haidar. *Revue Internationale de la Documentation*, XXIX (February 1962), 3-7.

Library Systems Analysis Guide, by Edward A. Chapman, Paul L. St. Pierre, and John Lubans. New York: Wiley-Interscience, a Division of John Wiley and Sons, Inc., 1970.

"Literary Unit Versus Bibliographic Unit," by Eva Verona. *Libri*, IX, No. 2 (1950), 79-104.

"The Machine and Cataloging," by George Piternick. *Advances in Librarianship*. Edited by Melvin J. Voigt. New York: Academic Press, 1970.

"Main Entries and Citations. One Test of the Revised Cataloging Code," by Elizabeth Lamb Tate. *Library Quarterly*, XXXIII (April 1963), 172-91.

"Main Entry: Principles and Counter-principles," by C. Sumner Spalding. *Library Resources and Technical Services*, XI (Fall 1967), 389-96.

"Name-title Entry Retrieval from a MARC File," by Philip L. Long and Frederick G. Kilgour. *Journal of Library Automation*, IV (December 1971), 211-12.

"A National Cataloguing Policy: Extracts from an Address Given by J. C. Downing, Assistant Editor, British National Bibliography and Secretary, Cataloguing and Indexing Group, at the London Seminar on the Implementation of the Anglo-American Cataloguing Rules, October 1968." *Catalogue and Index*, No. 13 (January 1969), 1, 16.

National Program for Acquisitions and Cataloging. Progress Report, No. 1— ; 1967— . Washington, D.C.: Library of Congress, Processing Department.

"Need for a New United States Code," by R. L. Angell. *Library Quarterly*, XXVI (October 1956), 318-30.

"New Catalog Code: The General Principles and the Major Changes," by F. Bernice Field. *Library Resources and Technical Services*, X (Fall 1966), 421-36.

New Rules for an Old Game, Proceedings of a Workshop on the 1967 Anglo-American Cataloguing Code Held by the School of Librarianship, the University of British Columbia, April 13 and 14, 1967. Edited by Thelma E. Allen and Daryl Ann Dickman. Vancouver: Publications Centre, University of British Columbia, 1967.

"The New Rules in Action: A Symposium." Edited by C. Donald Cook. *Library Resources and Technical Services*, XIII (Winter 1969), 7-41.

"On Searching Catalogs and Indexes with Inexact Title Information," by W. A. Hinkley. Unpublished M.A. thesis, University of Chicago Graduate Library School, 1968.

"Organization Theory and the Card Catalog," by Sister Robert Mary. *Library Resources and Technical Services*, VIII (Summer 1964), 329-33.

"Orthographic Error Patterns of Author Names in Catalog Searches," by Renata Tagliacozzo, Manfred Kochen and Lawrence Rosenberg. *Journal of Library Automation*, III (June 1970), 93-101.

"The Potential Usefulness of Catalog Access Points other than Author, Title, and Subject," by William S. Cooper. *Journal of the American Society for Information Science*, XXI (March-April 1970), 112-27.

Practical Handbook of Modern Library Cataloging, by William Warner Bishop. 2d ed. Baltimore: Williams and Wilkins Co., 1924.

Principles of Cataloging, Final Report, Phase I: Descriptive Cataloging, by Seymour Lubetzky. Los Angeles: Institute of Library Research, University of California, 1969.

The Printed Book Catalogue in American Libraries, by Jim Ranz. Chicago: American Library Association, 1964.

Problems of Recording Text Information in Machine Form for Use in a Scientific Information Communication Network, by Lawrence F. Buckland. Maynard, Mass.: Inforonics, Inc., 1966.

"Projet d'un code internationale de règles catalographiques," by Z. Tobolka. *Atti*, II, 121-52.

The Prussian Instructions; Rules for the Alphabetical Catalogs of the Prussian Libraries. Translated from 2d ed., 1908, with an introduction and notes by Andrew D. Osborn. Ann Arbor: University of Michigan Press, 1938.

"Rationalizing Title Added Entries," by Alice Charlton. *Journal of Cataloging and Classification*, VIII (March 1952), 27-30.

"Reaction of the Professional and Clerical Division of Cataloging Activities to Cataloging Courses," by S. G. Akers. *Library Quarterly*, V (January 1935), 101-36.

Readings in Library Cataloguing, by R. K. Olding, ed. Hamden, Conn.: Archon Books, 1966.

"Relationship of College and University Size to Library Adaptation of the 1967 Anglo-American Cataloging Rules," by Virginia Woll Atwood. *Library Resources and Technical Services*, XIV (Winter 1970), 69-83.

"Remarks in Proceedings for Forty-third Annual Meeting of the American Association of Law Libraries Held at Seattle, Washington, July 24-27, 1950," by W. B. Ellinger. *Law Library Journal*, XLIII (November 1950), 279-89.

"Remarks on LC Plans for Implementation of New Centralized Acquisitions and Cataloging Program under Title IIC, Higher Education Act," by John W. Cronin. *Library Resources and Technical Services*, XI (Winter 1967), 35-46.

Report of the Librarian of Congress, for the Fiscal Year Ending June 30, 1901. Washington, D.C.: Government Printing Office, 1901.

Report of the Librarian of Congress, for the Fiscal Year Ending June 30, 1935. Washington, D.C.: Government Printing Office, 1935.

Requirements Study for Future Catalogs, Progress Report No. 2. Chicago: University of Chicago Graduate Library School, 1968.

"The Research Worker's Approach to Books," by Ralph R. Shaw. *Acquisitions and Cataloging of Books.* Edited by William M. Rundall. Chicago: University of Chicago, 1949.

Review of *Anglo-American Cataloging Rules*, by Theodore C. Hines. *College and Research Libraries*, XXIX (January 1968), 62-63.

Review of *Anglo-American Cataloging Rules*, by Andre Nitecki. *American Documentation*, XVIII (October 1967), 255-57.

Review of *Anglo-American Cataloging Rules*, by Elizabeth Lamb Tate. *Library Quarterly*, XXXVII (October 1967), 394-95.

"Revising the Cataloguing Rules." *Catalogue and Index*, No. 15 (July 1969), 3.

"Revising the Rules." *Catalogue and Index*, No. 19 (July 1970), 3.

"Revising the Rules." *Catalogue and Index*, No. 20 (October 1970), 3.

Rules for a Dictionary Catalogue, by Charles A. Cutter. 4th ed. Washington, D.C.: Government Printing Office, 1904.

Rules for Compiling the Catalogues of Printed Books, Maps and Music in the British Museum. Revised ed. London. British Museum, 1936.

Rules for Descriptive Cataloging in the Library of Congress (adopted by the American Library Association). Washington: The Library of Congress, Descriptive Cataloging Division, 1949.

A Searcher's Manual, by George Lowy. Hamden, Conn.: Shoe String Press, 1965.

"The Selection, Processing and Storage of Nonprint Materials: A Critique of the Anglo-American Cataloging Rules as They Relate to Newer Media," by Jay E. Daily. *Library Trends*, XVI (October 1967), 283-89.

Seminar on the Anglo-American Cataloguing Rules (1967), Proceedings of the Seminar Organized by the Cataloguing and Indexing Group of the Library Association at the University of Nottingham, 22nd–25th March, 1968. Edited by J. C. Downing and N. F. Sharp. London: Library Association, 1969.

"Small Public Libraries and the Paris Conference," by David Remington. *Library Resources and Technical Services*, VIII (Summer 1964), 218-20.

Smithsonian Report on the Construction of Catalogues of Libraries, and their Publication by Means of Separate, Stereotyped Titles, by Charles Coffin Jewett. 2d ed. Washington, D.C.: Smithsonian Institution, 1853.

"Some Fundamental Principles in Cataloging," by Wyllis E. Wright. *Catalogers' and Classifiers' Yearbook*. Seventh Yearbook of the American Library Association, Catalog Section. Chicago: American Library Association, 1938.

Standard Bibliographic Description, a Proposal for a Standard Comprehensive International System for the Recording of Bibliographic Data–Revised Draft Proposal for Consideration by the IMCE Working Party on the Standard Bibliographic Description, by Michael Gorman. 1969. (Mimeographed.)

"Standards for Standards," by Richard W. Bird and Michael Gorman. *Catalogue and Index*, No. 6 (April 1967), 4-5.

A Study of Bengali Muslim Personal Names to Ascertain the Feasibility of Application of a Mechanistic Rule for Their Arrangement, by A. M. Abdul Huq. Pittsburgh: University of Pittsburgh Graduate School of Library and Information Sciences, 1970.

"Study of the Function of Title Added Entries for Non-fiction Books in the Dictionary Catalog," by M. E. Bridenstine. Unpublished M.L.S. thesis, University of Washington, 1953.

Study of the Rules for Entry and Headings in the 'Anglo-American Cataloging Rules, 1967 (British Text)', by Michael Gorman. London: Library Association, 1968.

"Systems Analysis and Computer Functions," by Paul J. Fasana. *Institute on Automation in Large Libraries: Implications for the Administration and the Manager, May 9-11, 1968*. Montreal: Ecole de Bibliotheconomie et Service d'education permanente, Universite de Montreal, 1968.

Technical Services in Libraries: Acquisitions, Cataloging, Classification, Binding, Photographic Reproduction, and Circulation Operations, by Maurice F. Tauber and associates. New York: Columbia University Press, 1953.

"The Three-dimensional Card Catalog," by Melvin B. Morgan. *Illinois Libraries*, XLII (September 1960), 445-46.

"A Time for Theory," by Bernard I. Palmer. *Catalogue and Index*, No. 6, (July 1967), 4.

"The Title Catalog: A Third Dimension," by Joseph Z. Nitecki. *College and Research Libraries*, XXIX (September 1968), 431-36.

"Title Entries: Are They a Waste of Time?" *New Zealand Libraries*, VIII (March 1945), 28-30.

"Title-Only Entries Retrieved by Use of Truncated Search Keys," by Frederick G. Kilgour, *et. al.*, *Journal of Library Automation*, IV (December 1971), 207-10.

"Titles: Fifth Column of the Catalog," by Seymour Lubetzky. *Library Quarterly*, XI (October 1941), 412-30.

Toward a Better Cataloging Code. Papers presented before the 21st Annual Conference of the Graduate Library School of the University of

Chicago, June 13-15, 1956. Chicago: University of Chicago Graduate Library School, 1957.

Tradition and Principle in Library Cataloguing, by Arthur Hugh Chaplin. Toronto: University of Toronto School of Library Science, 1968.

"A Truncated Search Key Title Index," by Philip L. Long and Frederick G. Kilgour. *Journal of Library Automation,* V (March 1972), 17-20.

"Types of Catalog Search and Their Relationship to Some Characteristics of the User," by Renata Tagliacozzo. *Integrative Mechanisms in Literature Growth.* Edited by Manfred Kochen. Report to the National Science Foundation, Vol. 2, Pt. IV. University of Michigan, Mental Health Institute, 1970.

"Unit Cataloging," by Valter Ahlstedt. *Libri,* I, No. 2 (1950), 113-70.

"Use of Secondary Entries for Titles in the Catalogs of Selected American Public Libraries," by Hope Isabel Adsit. Unpublished M.S. thesis, Columbia University, 1940.

"User Clues in Initiating Searches in a Large Library Catalog," by Ben-Ami Lipetz and Peter Stangl. *Proceedings of the American Society of Information Science,* V, 1968.

User Requirements in Identifying Desired Works in a Large Library, by Ben-Ami Lipetz. New Haven, Conn.: Yale University Library, 1970.

"White Elephants Revisted," by Maurice B. Line. *Catalogue and Index,* No. 13 (January 1969), 6.

INDEX

159